DEVELOPING DEPOSITION SKILLS

POLISI V. CLARK AND PARKER & GOULD

—SECOND EDITION—

MATERIALS FOR THE PLAINTIFF

DEVELOPING DEPOSITION SKILLS

POLISI V. CLARK AND PARKER & GOULD

—SECOND EDITION—

MATERIALS FOR THE
PLAINTIFF

ANTHONY J. BOCCHINO
Jack E. Feinberg Professor of Litigation

DAVID A. SONENSHEIN
I. Herman Stern Professor of Law

Temple University School of Law

NATIONAL INSTITUTE FOR TRIAL ADVOCACY

Bocchino, Anthony J. and David A. Sonenshein, *Developing Deposition Skills, Materials for the Plaintiff, Polisi v. Clark and Parker & Gould*, Second Edition (NITA, 2001)

ISBN: 978-1-55681-772-4

11/01

ACKNOWLEDGMENTS

We thank our colleagues, Professor Laura Little and Professor Alice Abreu for their invaluable assistance in the production of this case file. We also thank the participants in the inaugural class of Temple Law School's LL.M. in Trial Advocacy who worked through this file as part of their program and provided insight into improving the realism of the case file. We also are grateful to our Civil Procedure students who utilized another form of this case file and also provided helpful suggestions on its improvement.

Finally, we are indebted to Jerome Staller, Ph.D., and Stephanie Thomas, Ph.D., of the Center for Forensic Economic Studies in Philadelphia, who wrote the expert witness reports that appear in this file.

AJB
DAS

CONTENTS

SUPPLEMENTAL MATERIALS

INTRODUCTION

1. This is gender discrimination and defamation case based on a claim by the Plaintiff that she was denied partnership in the Defendant law firm, Parker & Gould (P & G), because she terminated a sexual relationship with the Defendant, Clark. She also claims gender discrimination based on a sexual harassment claim against the Defendant, Clark, and a hostile work environment claim against both Defendants.

2. This case file is designed for advanced advocacy training and involves difficult legal and factual issues for jury resolution. It also requires the examination of expert witnesses.

3. The parties have stipulated that all documents are authentic and meet the requirements of the Original Documents Rule. Other requirements for admissibility must be established by offering counsel.

4. This case file is completely fictitious and any resemblance to any person living or dead is coincidental and should not be misconstrued.

IN THE UNITED STATES DISTRICT COURT
FOR THE DISTRICT OF NITA

MARGARET POLISI	:	
	:	
Plaintiff	:	**CIVIL ACTION NO.**
	:	**YR-1-4678**
v.	:	
	:	
	:	**JURY TRIAL DEMANDED**
	:	
SIMON CLARK	:	
	:	
and	:	
	:	
PARKER & GOULD	:	
	:	
Defendants	:	

COMPLAINT

PARTIES

1.   Plaintiff, Margaret Polisi, is a female, adult individual, who is a citizen of Nita and of the United States. She resides in Nita City, Nita.

2(a).   Defendant, Parker & Gould, is a partnership organized under the laws of the State of Nita, engaged in the practice of law in Nita, with its offices at Four Independence Square, Nita City, Nita.

2(b).   Defendant, Parker & Gould, is an employer within the meaning of Section 701(b) of Title VII of the Civil Rights Act of 1964, as amended, 42 U.S.C. § 2000e(b), in that it engages in an industry affecting commerce and has had fifteen (15) or more employees for each working

1

day in each of twenty (20) or more calendar weeks in the current or pending calendar year.

3(a).   Defendant, Simon Clark, is a male, adult individual who is a citizen of Nita and the United States. He resides in Nita City, Nita.

3(b).   Defendant, Simon Clark, at all times material to this lawsuit, was and continues to be, a partner in the Defendant, Parker & Gould, and an agent of Parker & Gould within the meaning of 42 U.S.C. § 2000e(b).

JURISDICTION AND VENUE

4.   Plaintiff invokes this court's jurisdiction pursuant to 28 U.S.C. § 1331, 42 U.S.C. § 2000e-5(f)(3) and invokes Supplemental Jurisdiction pursuant to 28 U.S.C. § 1367. This action arises pursuant to 42 U.S.C. § 2000e et seq., Title VII of the Civil Rights Act of 1964, as amended.

5.   All conditions precedent to the filing of this action have been satisfied in that the Equal Employment Opportunity Commission of the United States issued its Right to Sue notice on December 28, YR-2.

6.   Venue is appropriate in the District of Nita because the defendants both reside in the State of Nita, the claims arose there, and the defendants may both be served with process there.

<h2 style="text-align:center">CLAIM I</h2>

Violation of the Civil Rights Act of 1964—Gender Discrimination

7.   Plaintiff graduated from Nita University Law School and passed the Nita bar examination in YR-9.

8.   In YR-9, Defendant, Parker & Gould, hired Plaintiff as a litigation associate in the law firm, where Plaintiff worked for seven years prior to her being forced to resign her position in the firm.

9.   In June of YR-3, Defendant Clark initiated a sexual relationship with the Plaintiff while she was an associate, working for him on the business of the Defendant, Parker and Gould.

10.   In January of YR-2, Plaintiff terminated the sexual relationship with Defendant, Clark.

11.   Although Plaintiff received excellent evaluations of her work over the period of her employment with Defendant, Parker & Gould, Plaintiff was rejected for partnership while male associates who were less qualified than Plaintiff were accepted for partnership with the Defendant, Parker & Gould, in YR-2.

12.   Plaintiff was rejected for partnership in the Defendant firm because she terminated a sexual relationship with her supervisor, Defendant, Simon Clark, in violation of Plaintiff's rights under Title VII of the Civil Rights Act of 1964, as amended, 42 U.S.C. § 2000e et seq.

CLAIM II

Violation of the Civil Rights Act of 1964 —

Quid Pro Quo Sexual Harassment

13.   Plaintiff incorporates by reference paragraphs 1 through 10 hereof, all of which amount to quid pro quo sexual harassment in violation of Title VII of the Civil Rights Act of 1964, 42 U.S.C. § 2000e, et seq.

CLAIM III

Violation of the Civil Rights Act of 1964 —

Hostile Working Environment

14.   Plaintiff incorporates by reference paragraph 1 through 11 hereof.

15.   Defendant Clark, while Plaintiff's supervisor, sexually harassed Plaintiff by, on numerous occasions, making unwelcome sexual advances to Plaintiff, culminating in a sexually intimate affair, all of which created and imposed on Plaintiff a sexually hostile and abusive working environment in violation of Plaintiff's rights pursuant to Title VII of the Civil Rights Act of 1964, as amended, 42 U.S.C. § 2000e, et seq.

WHEREFORE, Plaintiff prays that this Court will:

A.   Issue a declaratory judgment declaring that the actions of Defendants, Parker & Gould, and Clark, as set forth in this Complaint, violated Plaintiff's rights under Title VII of the Civil Rights Act of 1964, as amended, 42 U.S.C. § 2000e et seq.

B.   Enjoin and restrain Defendants Parker & Gould and Clark and all other persons acting on behalf of, or in concert with, them from engaging in such unlawful practices.

C.   Enter judgment in favor of Plaintiff, and against Defendants, Parker & Gould, and Clark, for back pay in the amount of wages and fringe benefits it is determined that Plaintiff lost as a result of Defendants' unlawful conduct, together with interest.

D.   Enter judgment in favor of Plaintiff and against Defendants, Parker & Gould, and Clark, reinstating plaintiff to the position she would have had absent Defendants' unlawful conduct. In the alternative, award plaintiff front pay in the amount of wages and benefits it is determined that Plaintiff is likely to lose because of Defendants' unlawful conduct.

E.   Enter judgment in favor of Plaintiff, and against Defendants for compensatory damages, including but not limited to, damages for mental anguish and humiliation, together with interest.

F.   Award Plaintiff reasonable attorneys' fees together with the costs of this action.

G.   Award such other and further legal and equitable relief as may be appropriate to redress fully the deprivation of Plaintiff's rights, to prevent their recurrence in the future and to protect other Parker & Gould employees from such unlawful behavior.

CLAIM IV

Defamation

16.   Plaintiff incorporates herein by reference paragraphs 1 through 15 hereof.

17.   Following the Plaintiff's rejection for partnership by the Defendant, Parker & Gould, Plaintiff applied for attorney positions with other law firms.

18.   When Defendant, Parker & Gould, was asked by at least two of the above-mentioned prospective employers for its opinion regarding Plaintiff's personality and abilities, Defendant, Clark, maliciously responded with false and slanderous statements, which defamed Plaintiff in her personal and professional reputation.

19.   The false statements made by Defendant, Clark, were made with the express, implied or apparent authority of Defendant, Parker & Gould, and Defendant, Parker & Gould, ratified those statements by not repudiating them.

20.   As a result of the false and slanderous statements maliciously made by Defendant, Clark, and ratified by Defendant, Parker & Gould, Plaintiff has suffered substantial emotional distress, mental anguish and pain and suffering; as well as damage to her personal and professional reputation and earning capacity.

WHEREFORE, Plaintiff demands judgment against Defendants, Parker & Gould, and

Clark, for compensatory damages in an amount in excess of $1,000,000.

JURY DEMAND

Plaintiff demands a jury trial for all claims triable by a jury.

Respectfully submitted,

David Darrow

David Darrow, Esquire
1500 Main Street
Nita City, Nita 10076

Dated: February 2, YR-1.

VERIFICATION

I, Margaret Polisi, am the plaintiff in the above-captioned action. I have read this complaint and verify that the allegations in it are true.

Margaret Polisi

Margaret Polisi, Esq.

Signed and sworn before me
this 2nd day of February, YR-1.

Karen Smith

Notary Public

IN THE UNITED STATES DISTRICT COURT
FOR THE DISTRICT OF NITA

MARGARET POLISI   :

              :

    Plaintiff   :   CIVIL ACTION NO.

              :   YR-1-4678

    v.   :

              :   **JURY TRIAL DEMANDED**

              :

SIMON CLARK   :

              :

   and   :

              :

PARKER & GOULD   :

              :

   Defendants   :

ANSWER OF
DEFENDANTS SIMON CLARK
and PARKER & GOULD

By way of answer, Defendants, Simon Clark and Parker & Gould, respond to Plaintiff's allegations as follows:

     1.   Admit.

     2(a).   Admit.

     2(b).   Admit.

     3(a).   Admit.

     3(b).   Admit.

     4.   Admit.

     5.   Admit.

6.   Admit.

7.   Admit.

8.   Admit the Defendant law firm hired Plaintiff as an associate in YR-9 and that Plaintiff worked at the firm for seven years before resigning her position.

9.   Deny that the Defendant Clark initiated the relationship. The relationship was mutually, freely and willingly entered into by the Plaintiff and the Defendant Clark.

10.   Admit.

11.   Admit that Plaintiff was rejected for partnership, but deny that Plaintiff received excellent evaluations over the period of her employment with the Defendant law firm.

12.   Denied.

13.   Deny all allegations incorporated by reference which were heretofore denied, and admit those allegations already admitted. Deny the allegation of quid pro quo sexual harassment.

14.   Deny all allegations incorporated by reference which were heretofore denied, and admit those allegations already admitted.

15.   Denied.

16.   Deny all allegations incorporated by reference which were heretofore denied, and admit those allegations already admitted.

17.   Defendants have insufficient knowledge to admit or deny.

18.   Denied.

19.   Denied.

20.   Denied.

For the Defendants,
       Simon Clark and
       Parker & Gould,

_____
Jane Jackson, Esq.

MATERIALS FOR THE
PLAINTIFFS

STATEMENT OF MARGARET POLISI

My name is Maggie Polisi. I live at 7010 Greenhill Rd. in Nita City. I am forty-one years old and the single parent of two children: Dave, who is twenty-one and a senior at Nita University, and Maureen, who is nineteen and a sophomore at Conwell College in the northwest part of the state. Until December 15th of YR-2, I was a lawyer with the firm of Parker & Gould in Nita City, at which time I was forced out of the law firm. Since then I have accepted a position as an Associate Professor of Law at Nita University School of Law where I teach Civil Procedure, Evidence, and a seminar in Complex Civil Litigation. I began this position as a tenure line faculty member in September of YR-1. During the spring semester, YR-1, I was an Adjunct Professor at the law school. I was hired as a full-time member of the faculty when a slot came open for the YR-1–YR-0 academic year.

I was born and raised in Wallingford, Connecticut, where I attended the public schools. In YR-23 I graduated from Lyman Hall High School and enrolled at the University of Pennsylvania in Philadelphia, where I majored in Political Science. During my freshman year I met Gregory Meyers, who was an MBA student at the Wharton School at Penn. We dated very seriously and in the spring of my freshman year, I became pregnant with my son, David. Greg and I married that summer, and he took a job with the Nita Fidelity Bank in their foreign investment division. I transferred from Penn to the University of Nita where I continued my studies.

My daughter, Maureen, was born in YR-19, one month after I graduated from Nita University. I was a good student and graduated summa cum laude and was elected to Phi Beta Kappa. Greg and I decided that it would be best for the kids if I stayed home with them while they were little, so I put my career on hold. As it turned out, Greg and I were not meant to be married to each other. His trips to Europe became longer and longer, and after a while, I didn't even mind. In YR-17, we divorced and Greg moved to Europe to work for an investment house there. I needed to work to help support my kids, but also to keep my sanity.

Given my undergraduate degree in political science, I had no particular job skills. I always had an interest in the law, so at the encouragement of a good friend of mine, I applied to a number of law firms to work as a paralegal. I received a number of offers, but chose to go with Parker & Gould. P & G appeared to be the most flexible in terms of giving me time to care for my kids when I was needed. They were also willing to assign me to cases that did not take me out of town for anything more that a night or two. They understood that I was a single mother, and that to send me out of town was a hardship. No other firm was willing to give me such assurances, so I went with P & G.

P & G is a large law firm that does the full range of legal work available in the city. The firm now has approximately 330 lawyers, seventy-five of whom are partners. At the time I went to work for P & G as a paralegal, it was one of the largest law firms in Nita City, but only had about seventy-five lawyers. I was assigned to the litigation section of the firm. The firm also has a corporate section, a tax section, and an estates section.

I did work for many of the partners at the firm, but in YR-15 I was assigned to work on a large commercial case involving several of the biggest banks in Nita City. The partner in charge of that case was Simon Clark, and I worked very closely with him and with Cliff Fuller (who at the time was a midlevel associate with the firm) for a period of approximately two years. By the time the case came to trial, in January of YR-13, I was selected as one of the trial paralegals to work on the case. Simon was apparently pleased with my work because I received a substantial bonus and a pay raise when we won the case at trial, and settled it very favorably in lieu of an appeal.

Simon Clark has always had a reputation in the firm as a womanizer. I was warned by a number of the more senior paralegals as well as some of the women associates to watch out for him when I joined the firm. They told me that Simon was in a very unhappy marriage, and that he used this fact as an entreé with a number of women in the office, both paralegals and lawyers. Apparently he had promised a number of young women that he would leave his wife to be with them, but that never happened. In the end, the women would either quit the firm or be fired, and Simon would go on to his next conquest.

I'll have to admit, that during the bank case in YR-15 through YR-13, I worked very closely with Simon for long hours and in close quarters, and he never really came on to me. There was some innocent flirting on his part, but maybe because of his reputation, or maybe because he reminded me of my husband, I steered clear of him. I don't know if he was interested in a personal relationship with me at the time, but as I said, I never really responded to his flirting and he never made any inappropriate advances other than from time to time, when talking with me, he would touch me. For example, when he was reading something over my shoulder, he would put his hands on my shoulders. Although this bothered me, I never said anything because, after all, he was the boss and even though I was uncomfortable with the physical contact, it did not seem to be overtly sexual in nature.

As it turned out, he apparently was involved with a woman associate at the firm, one who was also working on the case. Her name is Susan McGinty. Susan left the firm some time after the bank case. I understand that she now practices law in Philadelphia. The word is that when

Simon refused to leave his wife, Susan put her foot down, and the end result was that she was forced to leave the firm.

During the bank case, Simon was very complimentary of my work. He often said things to the effect that I was the equal of many of the associates who were working on the case. Once he even kidded Cliff Fuller in front of me that I was going to take Cliff's place. In fact, it was Simon Clark who encouraged me to attend law school. He recommended that I leave the firm and go to school full time, but by that time, my ex-husband's child support payments were sporadic at best, and it was an economic necessity for me to continue to work. I applied to, and was accepted, as an Evening Division law student at Nita University School of Law and began classes in the fall of YR-13. Both Simon and Cliff (who was a graduate of Nita law school) wrote letters of recommendation for me. I'm sure they were helpful because my application was a little late and I still was accepted.

I continued to work at P & G during my law school years. The firm was very good about accommodating my law school schedule, and allowed me to take some time off during exams and make it up later. I also was given permission to use the law firm facilities for my research and writing projects during non-work hours. During the entire time I was in law school Simon Clark showed a good deal of interest in me and my legal career. When I made Dean's list in my first semester of law school he was very complimentary and offered to take me out to dinner to celebrate. Because I was so busy, between work, school, and my kids, I turned him down for dinner, but did agree to go to lunch. At lunch he was very charming and appeared to be genuinely interested in me, my kids, and my career. He said that I should be sure to make some time for myself and although this was good advice, the time just wasn't there.

Simon's apparent professional interest in me continued throughout my law school career. He was always available to discuss a problem I had with my law school work, or with a case I was working on at the firm. Although his habit of touching on the arm or shoulder when we were talking embarrassed me, I never said anything to him because the touching, although unwanted, was not, as I said earlier, overtly sexual. After my first year at law school, during which I achieved top 5 percent grades, I was promoted in the firm to a position as a law clerk. The work I did as a law clerk in the beginning was not much different than my paralegal work, but as I became more sophisticated in the law, so did my assignments. Although I did not receive formal evaluations as a law clerk at P & G, I was rehired each year, and my pay was increased on a regular basis.

In addition, unlike most of the law clerks, I did receive bonuses each year. It was explained to me that since I would have received bonuses as a paralegal, that the firm had decided that I would continue to be part of the bonus compensation program at the firm. To tell you the truth, I was quite surprised when I did receive a bonus at the end of the year in which I became a law clerk, because I knew that the law clerks did not normally get bonuses. I was given my bonus check by Simon Clark. I remember that I had just had to do some roof repairs on my small house, and that it looked like we were going to have a lean Christmas when he gave me the check. The bonus was something like $2,000 and it could not have come at a better time. I was so excited that I gave Simon a big hug. I remember he made some comment like, "with that reaction, I wish we could have given you more." What he said embarrassed me, but I really didn't think much of it the time. I just let go of him, and thanked him. He told me that he had gone to bat for me on the bonus, and that I was the only law clerk to receive one. I thanked him again, and that was that.

I did very well in law school. I always made Dean's list, and according to the percentile rankings, my grades were always in the top 5 percent which was the highest percentile reported. I was selected for the law review. I had a note published in my second year, a comment published in my third year and in my fourth year, I was selected to be one of the Articles Editors.

During the four years of law school, I did some assignments on Simon Clark's cases and he always seemed to be pleased with my work. He did ask me out to dinner on a number of occasions to either celebrate some success of mine at the law school or the winning of a case of his that we worked on together. I always declined because of my schedule, but we did go out to lunch several times. Simon would flirt with me, telling me how attractive I was or by making comments like "if I weren't a married man, I'd be camped out at your doorstep," and "if I were only ten years younger, I'd fly away with you to a desert island." Although I was embarrassed by his behavior, I just put it off to his being from another era, and just sloughed him off by making a little joke or ignoring him. Also, because I thought that, even though his comments were embarrassing to me, he did not mean anything by the comments, I thought that any protest on my part would look silly, and he might view me as an "hysterical woman."

During the four years I was at the law school, Simon Clark's stock rose steadily with the firm. He was obviously one of the firm's best litigators and trial lawyers, and was very well regarded professionally within the firm. It was generally known in the firm that Simon was responsible for attracting and keeping some of the firm's best clients. It was probably because of his talent that his extramarital affairs with both paralegals and associates were so easily tolerated. It might also have been that the firm didn't care about his personal life, so long as he continued to succeed as a lawyer. I really can't understand why the firm put up with his behavior, but it did. At any rate, the rumors of his philandering never ceased, and Simon went through a number of fairly public affairs within the firm while I was in law school.

I know for a fact that he had a six-month relationship with Ellen Dorsen, who was a paralegal with the firm. This was in YR-12. She spoke openly of her weekends with Simon, and the places they went together. When the affair ended, Ellen took it quite hard. A number of the other paralegals were very hard on her, given the way she flaunted her relationship with Simon, and it affected her work. She was eventually fired by the firm. I also know that Simon had affairs with two women associates, Karen Newman in YR-11, and Carol Merritt in YR-10. I know this because they were assigned to work on two different cases with Simon, both of which I was assigned to as a law clerk.

Karen was a third-year associate and in her late twenties at the time of her fling with Simon. She initially sort of took the whole thing in stride. When the affair ended after about a month, she confided in me about it. She said that Simon had made some statements about leaving his wife, but that Karen knew he was lying, so she ended the relationship. Over the next several months Karen complained to me, and anyone else who would listen, about how her work assignments had gotten pretty bad and that rather than being assigned to the high profile commercial cases, as she had been in the recent past, she was being asked to work on some divorce matters for some of our business clients. She also complained that she was having a hard time keeping her billable hours up because she wasn't getting assigned enough work. I know one of the people she complained to at the time was Cliff Fuller, who by that time was a well-respected young partner at the firm, and was known to be Simon Clark's protege.

The divorce cases were not considered great cases in the firm at that time because they were only handled because the client was a business client, not because the firm valued this type of practice. Karen held on for about six months, but eventually left the firm for a job with a smaller firm. At the time she told me that she believed that her dumping Simon was the reason for her bad assignments or lack of assignments and that she decided to leave the firm before "they" could damage her reputation. At the time I thought she was overreacting, but given what happened to me, my guess is she did the right thing for herself at the time. I have seen Karen every once in a while since she left the firm. When this whole thing happened to me, she somehow heard about it and asked me to lunch. She commiserated with me. Her basic comment was that Simon appeared to be up to his old tricks. Although she didn't name names, she told me there were a number of women (either paralegals or lawyers) in the city who had been forced out of P & G after their relationships ended with Simon Clark.

Carol Merritt's situation was more complicated. At the time she started her affair with Simon, she was a fourth-year associate, about thirty years old, and married. She fell head over heels in love with Simon while working on a case with him. Their affair lasted a good six months. About three months into the affair, she got so serious that she left her husband. I had a conversation with her about Simon before she left her husband, and warned her about Simon's reputation. I even suggested she contact Karen Newman or talk to Cliff Fuller. She assured me that Simon was going to leave his wife and marry her; that he was just waiting for the right time, but that it would be soon. As it turned out, Simon never did leave his wife, and when the case they were working on together ended, he terminated his relationship with Carol abruptly. Carol ended up taking about a month off, and came back to the firm only long enough to pack up her office and move out. I found out she was leaving from Rachel Levin, who was Charles Milton's secretary with whom I was friendly at the time. I talked to Carol at Rachel's suggestion. She thanked me for trying to be a good friend when I warned her about Simon. She also told me that her husband had taken her back and that the two of them were moving to Washington, D.C. She said that even though Simon had been a jerk, that he had given her a great recommendation, and that she was going to work for a good firm in D.C.

I think that Carol's, as well as Karen's experiences, were consistent with Simon Clark's normal behavior. I don't think that he is an evil man, but I do think that he does evil things. He has a fatal flaw in that he cannot be satisfied with one woman, or at least, not for long. But when he's done with them, or they're done with him, he doesn't want them around. I don't know whether he knows or cares about how devastating being treated like that can be. My conclusions about Simon are a result of learning some hard lessons from my relationship with him, and I certainly didn't appreciate these things about Simon back then. While I was in law school, I viewed Simon and his affairs as just a fact of life, and while I had some sympathy for the women who got involved with him, they were adults and they knew his reputation, so what happened to them seemed to be something they should have suspected.

For me, with the exception of the mild flirtations and the unwanted but relatively innocuous touching, Simon Clark was a hero. He was one of the best lawyers in the firm, especially for his age. During the time I was in law school Simon was in his late thirties and early forties. I saw him examine witnesses and he was a master. His legal mind was brilliant. He always was able to make me understand the most complicated of concepts as if they were obvious. He also took the time to congratulate me on my successes in law school and to give me a "well done" on the work I did for him. And although this now seems so inconsistent with his treatment of women, he was one of the most active volunteer lawyers in the firm who did pro-bono work for the ACLU. To say that I admired him is an understatement. I considered him to be a role model and as my mentor. After all, it was Simon who encouraged me to go to law school, and, in fact, it was Simon and Cliff Fuller, for whom I did quite a bit of work, who are most responsible for my becoming an associate with P & G.

No one who worked as a law clerk during the school year, and no one who was a graduate of the evening division of Nita University School of Law, had, as of YR-9, ever been offered a position as an associate at P & G. There were people in the firm, like Cliff Fuller, who were graduates of Nita University, but no one from the evening division. Virtually all of the associates came through the Summer Associates program, wherein approximately twenty to twenty-five of the best and brightest students from around the country, and from the "best" law schools are brought in for ten weeks during the summer between their second and third year of law school. Thus, I was surprised when Simon Clark and Cliff Fuller came by my office one day, early in the fall of my fourth year of law school, and invited me to lunch to "talk about my future with the firm." At the time, Cliff was a relatively new partner (but generally considered a rising star and the protege of Simon Clark) and a very active member of the hiring committee. Simon was the chair of the hiring committee.

At lunch, they said that they had noted that I had not applied for an associate's position, and asked why. I told them that the reason should be obvious: that the firm had never hired a law clerk and never hired someone from the evening division of the Nita Law School, so that it seemed pointless to do so. They both said that they had both been very impressed with my work, that it was the equivalent of any of the summer associates, and that while it wasn't a foregone conclusion that I would be hired, they thought I should apply and that they would both enthusiastically support my application. To say that I was flattered would be an understatement. I had always harbored a fantasy that I'd somehow get to be a lawyer at P & G, but I never expected it could happen.

Simon and Cliff asked where else I had applied and I told them the names of the firms. Because, at the time, there was still some bias against evening-division graduates in some of the largest firms (including P & G), I had applied to what was generally considered the second tier of firms in the city. They were very good law firms, but did not have the size or the clout of the top firms like P & G. I nonetheless followed through on my interviews with those firms, and given P & G's interest, even applied to some of the other large firms in the city, several of which offered me interviews.

I, of course, followed through on Simon and Cliff's suggestion and applied to P & G. Although I was nervous, I must have had a good preliminary interview, because I was invited to an interview with the entire hiring committee. That interview seemed to go even better. The only partner who seemed negative towards me was one of the few women partners in the firm, Jayne Post. Jayne was a relatively new partner at the time, and she was trying to set up a permanent domestic relations section within the firm. At that point she was the only partner doing that work almost exclusively and she had three associates, two of whom were women and one an African-American man, working for her.

I had told the committee that I was most interested in a commercial litigation practice, but that I needed to be assigned to work on cases that were primarily based in Nita City. Ms. Post seemed quite negative in response to my statement that it would be necessary for me to be assigned to work on Nita-based cases (as opposed to being sent across country for months at a time), because of my children. At that point David was twelve and Maureen was ten (going on thirty-five) and they needed a lot of my attention. Ms. Post seemed to suggest that it was inappropriate for me to ask for special consideration in assignments, and although it might have been, it would have been pointless for me to take a job that would take me away from my kids for an extended period of time, because that would have been impossible. I wanted to be upfront about what I needed in terms of job flexibility. Prior to my interviews, I didn't know how the committee would react, so I had run my problem by Cliff Fuller. Cliff later told me that he had talked it over with Simon Clark and that Simon didn't see a problem. After all, the firm had always accommodated me in my work as a paralegal, and eventually the kids would be out on their own.

As it turned out, P & G was the most receptive to my particular needs of all the law firms from whom I received offers, Jayne Post notwithstanding. Even though I received offers from five other firms, including one other silk-stocking firm, I ended up going with P & G, partially because of their flexibility, but mostly because I considered their offer an honor. On the day I accepted P & G's offer, Simon Clark came by my office. Although I thought it was a little inappropriate, he gave me a big hug and welcomed me aboard. He made me a little uncomfortable, but I was so happy to be hired by P & G, and because he had helped me to get the position, I just thanked Simon for all the help he had given me. He told me that he'd be sure to ask for me on some of his cases so that we could work closely together. To be honest, I was flattered.

I finished out the year as a law clerk and graduated in YR-9 from law school, and received a number of academic awards and prizes at graduation. I am providing you with a copy of my resume which contains those awards. I graduated magna cum laude, and was ranked first in the evening division class. (SEE EXHIBIT 1)

I received my official letter of appointment from P & G in July of YR-9. (SEE EXHIBIT 2) It contained some general language about my job duties that caused me some pause in that there was no mention of my understanding that I would not be assigned to cases that would take me out of Nita City for extended periods of time. I mentioned this to Simon Clark and he told me not to be concerned, that the letter was just a form letter and that the firm understood my need to be near my children.

After taking the bar exam, I started work as an associate at P & G in September of YR-9. I was assigned to the litigation section as I had requested, and started off in the library with the rest of my colleagues in my associates class. My beginning salary was $85,000. Partially because of my years of experience as both a paralegal and a law clerk, and partially because, as I now realize, I have some talent, I seemed to progress a little faster than some of the other associates in my class. It also helped, I think, that I was older and had gone to law school while working full time and having the responsibility of being a single parent. Because I had some maturity, the stress of the job had less effect on me than it did on the typical first-year associate.

To be honest, my workload at P & G as an associate seemed less than my workload as a law clerk and a law student. In addition, because I was comfortable with the working environment at P & G and knew all the little administrative things that you need to know to survive, I spent a lot less time spinning my wheels. In addition, the concept of keeping time, which was new for most of my colleagues, most of whom were fresh from law school and twenty-five years old, was common to me and also presented no obstacle to my doing my best work.

I was assigned to work on a wide variety of commercial litigation matters and worked with a number of partners. I did very little work with Simon Clark during the first five years of my time at P & G. I did an occasional memo, but I never worked a complete case from start to finish with him. That may have been just happenstance, but it may also have been because of my desire to not become involved in cases that involved a lot of travel for extended periods. P & G has a national practice and Simon was considered to be the best litigator and trial lawyer in the firm, so he was always handling the most important commercial litigation cases for the firm. When those cases were in litigation, he and his litigation team would spend months at a time in the part of the country where the case took place interviewing and deposing witnesses, orchestrating other discovery and making and responding to motions. If the case went to trial, no matter where the trial, Simon was likely to be the lead trial lawyer. As a result, he was frequently out of the office for extended periods of time, so the opportunities to work for him were limited.

When I did work for Simon, our working relationship was good, and except for an occasional comment about how I looked, he was very professional. In fact, the rumors about Simon and his law firm romances were less frequent. Not that I sought out such rumors, but they seemed less frequent and I don't know of any particular affair he had during the period of YR-9 through YR-3. I know that Simon's son was almost killed in a car accident during that period, and maybe that caused him to focus on his family life, I don't know. Whenever I was assigned to one of Simon's cases, he was always complimentary of my work.

The partner I did the most work for at P & G during the period of YR-9 through YR-4 was Cliff Fuller. In the beginning, Cliff requested that I work with him on some of his smaller commercial litigation cases. While some of my fellow associates preferred the big cases because there was more importance attached to them in the firm, I was interested in getting some work on cases where I could actually get experience doing something other than research and writing. By working with Cliff on relatively smaller cases in terms of amounts involved, where there were fewer associates assigned, I got a fuller look at the litigation of a case because I was involved in virtually all aspects of the case. In addition, I developed an excellent working relationship with Cliff, and because he had confidence in my abilities, he allowed me to take more responsibility in litigation than many of my colleagues in my associates class were getting in their cases. Cliff made sure I got experience in taking and defending depositions as well as motion practice, including oral arguments.

Cliff also made certain that I did work on some of the more prestigious matters in the law firm, for political purposes. He counseled me that it was necessary for an associate to become known for doing good work, on big cases, to progress in the firm. In terms of firm politics, big cases for big clients had the most currency, and so a job well done in one of those cases did much more for your reputation in the firm than an equally good job on a lesser case (involving less money or for a less important client). This is the sort of thing that, but for the guidance of Cliff Fuller, I never would have appreciated.

Cliff also counseled me to avoid getting involved in the domestic relations cases that were handled by Jayne Post and her subgroup within the litigation section. Ms. Post had actually built a rather thriving domestic relations practice within the firm. By YR-4, she had two other partners and four associates who worked primarily with her in her cases. From time to time she would need some extra help taking depositions or writing trial memoranda and would ask for volunteers among the associates to help out. Because I was marginally interested in the work and because Ms. Post was one of only two women partners in the litigation section during my early years with the firm, I did volunteer from time to time to do some work for her. She was very demanding, but I found her comments on my performance fair and helpful. Cliff warned me that my stock in the firm would be lessened if I became too identified with that kind of practice. Because he was such a good friend and mentor, I followed his advice, and never did a major assignment for her. On one occasion, in YR-3, Ms. Post asked for me to do some work on one of her complicated divorce cases, involving the equitable distribution of a number of businesses, but because I was extremely busy on another case that was getting ready for trial, I was unable to accept the assignment and it was given to another associate. I know that Ms. Post was offended by my not taking on the assignment, but it was really out of my control.

During the period of YR-9 through YR-5, as in every year at P & G, my job performance was evaluated. As I understood the process, the chair and the deputy chair of the litigation section solicited comments from all those partners for whom I worked during the year. During that period of time the chair of the litigation section was Charles Milton and his deputy was Ted Potter, both of whom I had worked for on their cases over the years. I then had a meeting with them, which was held close in time to my anniversary date with the firm, which in my case was September, wherein they reviewed my progress with the firm. During that meeting I was given a grade. The scale was A to F. After I was given my grade, I was given what I assumed was a compilation of the comments that were made about me, and told how the firm would like to see me improve in the upcoming year. These comments appeared to be coming from a file with my name on it. You have shown me some memoranda that refer to my evaluations, and although I have no way of remembering if they track what was said to me in my evaluations, they certainly could. They are accurate concerning my billable hours for each year. (SEE EXHIBITS 3A–3G) I was also told how many other associates in my law school class received the same grade as me, or higher. I was then told what my raise would be for the next year. The raise was pegged to the grade you received. An A got you a 7 percent raise, a B got 5 percent, a C got 3 percent. I don't know if there was any raise associated with a D because I never got one. I was never given anything in writing during any of my evaluations except that I received a written confirmation of my raise. (SEE EXHIBITS 4A–4F).

In my first evaluation, in YR-8, I was given the grade of C and was told that there were two people in my class of twenty associates who received the grade of B and eight who received the grade of C. The remainder received D grades. Although I was warned that the normal grade for an associate in the first year was a C or D, because I never had received a grade in school lower than a B I was a little taken aback. I was told that the partners for whom I worked were generally happy with my work, but that I needed to work on being more concise in my writing style. I was also told that my billable hours were okay, but that there were others who were billing more hours. I was later approached by Cliff Fuller, who assured me that my work was just fine, and that I should just keep plugging and that I would be all right.

I was determined in my next evaluation to improve, and I did. In YR-7 through YR-5, I was graded as a B. In YR-7, there were three other associates in my class with the grade of B, in YR-6, three other B's, and in YR-5, four other associates were graded as high as a B. There were no A's given any of the associates in our class in the litigation section during our first four years, but as I understand it, that was not unusual. I guess they just wanted to keep us working. There must have been some low grades however, because by YR-5, our class of associates was dwindling. Of the twenty people who started with my class, there were eleven remaining in YR-5. Most people had gone on to other firms, either within Nita City or in other states. One person, Gary Sherman, who was considered one of the brightest and most talented associates in our class, took a teaching position at the University of Conwell Law School in the northwest part of the state. And two people who were interested in getting some actual courtroom trial experience had gone to the U.S. Attorney's office in Nita City.

Each of the oral evaluations in YR-7 through YR-5, were, for the most part, complimentary. There seemed to be a consensus that my research and writing skills were quite good, and really needed no improvement. Apparently there was one partner in each of these evaluations who questioned my analytical skills, but I was not given any specific examples of where my analytical skills were lacking. I was told by Cliff Fuller not to worry about that particular comment, because it was from a partner who thought that because I was an evening division graduate that I could not be as smart as the other associates. Cliff said that although this opinion was unfair, that I should just ignore it and he confided in me that when he was an associate that he got similar comments, just because he was the first University of Nita law school graduate to join P & G. I don't know if Cliff was telling me the truth about his receiving bad evaluations, but given his reputation in the firm as one of the best and the brightest, he sure made me feel better.

Another negative comment that I received in one evaluation, I think it was in YR-5, was that because I was unavailable to travel on cases for extended periods of time, due to my child care responsibilities, that I was somehow not fulfilling my obligations to the firm. I remember talking with Rachel Levin, a friend from my paralegal days, and Milton's secretary about the comment and she encouraged me to talk to Milton about it. She said he was fair. I reminded

Charles Milton and Ted Potter that I had made clear when I was hired that my travel was limited, and that the firm had hired me nonetheless, and that I therefore thought the comment was unfair.

Q: Did you ever talk to Milton about that issue again?

A: Yes, I was later called back into Charles Milton's office, and it was explained to me that the comment about not traveling had been made by a woman partner who felt that my children were old enough to be left with a childcare provider in the home if I needed to be out of town for an extended period of time.

Q: What was your reaction to what Milton had to say?

A: I think that somehow they thought that because the comment was made by a woman, that it was fair.

Q: What did you say to Milton?

A: I again stated that I had come to the firm with an understanding that my travel would be limited.

Q: How did he respond?

A: He didn't really. With that, the conversation was terminated.

Q: Just like that?

A: He wasn't rude or anything, but he got a phone call and told me that he had to take the call and asked that I excuse him, so I left the office.

Q: Was anything else said to you by Milton about the issue of your traveling on firm business?

A: No, it never came up again with him.

The only women partners in the litigation section at the time I worked at the firm were Jayne Post, Sherry Barker, and Ann Feinman who worked in the domestic relations unit and Cheryl Stein who worked primarily in bankruptcy litigation. Because I had not worked for anyone other that Ms. Post, I assume that the comment came from her, even though I never was asked to do any extended travel by her. As I said, I rarely did any work for her at all.

The only other negative comment that I received in my first four evaluations was that "I was not aggressive enough" and that I lacked "toughness." When I asked for specific examples, none were forthcoming, but it was a consistent comment. I spoke with Cliff Fuller about those comments as well. I remember specifically having a conversation with him after my YR-5 evaluation, and he said that the "lack of aggressiveness" was a common comment made about women associates by older male partners and that I shouldn't be overly concerned about it. He said that the times were changing, but slowly, and the fact that Cheryl Stein had made partner in the litigation section in YR-6 to work in the bankruptcy subgroup was a good sign for my future. He also pointed out that it looked like women in both the tax and corporate sections would be made partner in that year.

My fifth year at the firm was a particularly difficult one for me. In the fall of YR-5 my father was diagnosed as having pancreatic cancer. He only lived for two months after being diagnosed (he died in November of YR-5) and I spent a lot of time traveling from Nita City back home to Connecticut. The travel, plus the emotional upheaval, affected my work, both in terms of quantity and quality. Cliff Fuller, who by that time was the deputy chair of the litigation section (Simon Clark was the chair), approached me with some complaints. When I told him what I was going through, he was sympathetic, but told me to use my work as a refuge so that I didn't adversely affect my future with the firm.

That year was also the year that David was a junior in high school and Maureen was a freshman. David got involved with a bad group of kids. His grades in the first and second quarter were well below normal; he was a solid B+/A student and his grades were in the C range for those quarters. Eventually, I caught him with some marijuana in his room. We spent a lot of time working through that problem and he seemed to respond pretty well, and by the third quarter his grades were into the B+ range and by the end of his junior year he was back on track with good grades.

Maureen went through the classic teenage problems that all young girls face during that first year of high school. It was especially difficult for us, because there was no father there to help her through that time when teenage girls want nothing to do with their mothers. Nonetheless, we weathered the storm and by the summer of YR-4, we were once again a functioning family.

The effect of all of this was that my billable hours were down for that year and the quality of my work also suffered. Even Cliff Fuller was less than complimentary about my work. I was trying hard, but with my personal problems, I was just not functioning at anywhere near my normal level.

My firm evaluation for that year reflected the kind of year I had. The evaluation was held in Simon Clark's office. Simon had been made the chair of the litigation section of the firm in the fall of YR-4. Cliff Fuller was also there as the deputy chair. Simon told me that although he and Cliff had fought very hard for me, and had asked that my personal problems be considered, that my grade for my fifth year was a C. They said that there was one associate who received an A and two associates who received B's and three other associates who received C's. They told me that my hours were not acceptable and that for the first time, they had received some substantial complaints about the quality of my work. They both said that they believed that I was partnership material and that I had what it took to make partner, but that my C grade was a real problem.

Simon told me that I had basically three ways to go. First, I could look for a job with another firm, and that the firm would be very complimentary of me in giving recommendations. One of the associates who received a C took this option. Second, he could arrange for a very good position for me in the general counsel's office of Nita Computer World, which was one of the firm's best corporate clients. He said that two other associates who were graded at C had chosen to take the option of going to work with a client company, but that the Nita Computer World job was the best such position available. Third, I could come to work with him on a major piece of antitrust litigation that was just gearing up on behalf of Nita Computer World, work like hell, and repair my reputation within the firm.

To me, there was no choice. I chose to go to work on the Nita Computer World (NCW) litigation with Simon Clark. I was not a quitter and I had worked too hard to leave P & G under a cloud. I knew that many other former associates with P & G had gone to work for the firm's clients and that the jobs had great security and benefits, but I wasn't willing, at that time in my life, to settle for such a job. Simon said that he knew that I would choose the third option, but made it clear that my career with P & G was on the line and that he expected my best work on the case. There were two young partners assigned to the case and four other associates. I was the senior associate on the NCW case.

The work on the NCW case was the most challenging and rewarding legal work I had ever done. I use many of the things I learned during that litigation in the teaching of my complex litigation seminar at the law school. The case, which involved an allegation of price fixing on the part of NCW and other distributors of computer hardware and software, was complicated and presented fascinating legal and tactical issues. Simon was right, though. The hours were long and exhausting, and because so much was on the line, both for me personally, and for the client, I worked harder than I had ever worked before. This was especially so because the judge set a very quick discovery deadline of six months, and set the case for a firm trial date in June of YR-3.

Because I was the senior associate on the case, I helped prepare the partners for depositions, drafted all motions and supporting memoranda for use by the partners (who made any necessary additions or corrections), and was allowed to conduct some of the peripheral depositions myself. I was involved in all aspects of case planning and litigation strategy. The NCW case only increased my admiration for Simon Clark as a lawyer. His insights were incredible, his instincts sharp and his ability to get information, both through document production and depositions was nothing short of brilliant in my opinion.

As I said, I was involved in all aspects of the litigation. I often times traveled with Simon or one of the other partners for depositions both in and out of the state. The travel wasn't all that frequent and usually did not involve more than two or three days away from home in a row, so I agreed to the travel. Even though I was a little nervous about leaving the kids, David was being very responsible, having received an early acceptance into the honors program and a partial academic scholarship at Nita University, and Maureen, after her bad year, seemed to be doing very well both academically and otherwise. In addition, I knew that my career was on the line, so the travel, even though not optimal, was necessary.

It was on one of these trips out of town, in January of YR-3, that Simon Clark made his first sexual proposition to me. After a particularly grueling day of depositions and a long preparation session in his room, Simon ordered up a late night meal with some wine and we sat and relaxed. Talk turned to our personal lives. Simon asked about the kids and I told him they were doing well. He then asked how I was doing. I told him how happy I was working on the NCW case, and he said that my work was first-rate and that my prospects for partnership were looking better every day. He then asked about my social life, and although it was none of his business, I told him that between the job and the kids, I had no social life. Simon then started talking about his marriage and his kids. He said that he and his wife were married only in name, and that they only stayed married for his children, the youngest of whom was a high school senior.

Although I was uncomfortable with the conversation, I was exhausted from work, and the closeness of our working relationship made the conversation come pretty easily. Simon then made some comment about how different I was from his wife. He said that she seemed to care about nothing other than her social standing and really cared little for him or their children. He said that he admired me for what I had accomplished, both professionally and with my children. At some point during the conversation he got up and walked around the back of my chair and started to massage my shoulders. Although this made me more than a little uncomfortable, I'll have to admit that it felt good, so I didn't protest. He then kissed me on the neck. Although I shouldn't have been, given Simon's reputation, I was surprised and I jumped up out of my chair.

Simon seemed shocked by my reaction, but I just said that I wasn't ready for that kind of relationship, and that I should probably leave. He told me that there was no need for that, that he was attracted to me, but that he had misread my signals. He apologized for being so forward. I sat back in the chair and we talked about the case and the next day's deposition for about a half hour. I then went back to my room.

The next day Simon was very cool and formal with me. I guess I must have bruised his ego. I assumed that things would get back to normal between us as the case continued at its breakneck pace and after a couple of more days of the silent treatment, our working relationship was back to normal. In March, we were out of town on another set of depositions, and again were meeting in his room after a day of depositions. After we finished our business, Simon asked if I was interested in a little relaxation and conversation. When I hesitated, he said something like "just conversation," and I relaxed and agreed to share a late supper and a glass of wine with him.

Simon was particularly talkative, and after inquiring after my family and me, he started to talk about his relationship with his family. He again complained about his wife having more concern for her country club and social gatherings than him and his children. He told me that his marriage that had lasted over twenty-five years had been nothing more than a shell for the last fifteen. He asked me if I was aware of the rumors about him and other women and I admitted that I was. He didn't deny them, but explained them away as his searching for something better. He then told me that once his son graduated from high school that June, that he was going to file for divorce. He said that he had thought about divorce before, but that when he talked to his wife that she made it very clear that he would have a hard time seeing the children, and that she would use his affairs to ensure that his access to the children was severely limited. According to Simon, his relationship with his children was strained at best, because of his long hours at work and long periods of time away from home, and he didn't want to lose what little relationship he had with them.

He also said that when he was younger he worried about the effect a divorce would have on his career, given that many of his corporate clients were controlled by social friends who were originally friends of his wife and her family. He said that he now understood that although social relationships may open doors, that corporate decisions are made on sound business bases, not on social friendship. He was now confident, or so he said, that his clients would remain with him regardless of whether he and his wife divorced, so that he was ready to go forward with the divorce. In fact, he said, the only thing that kept him going was his work; that his only regret was that he didn't have someone special to share it with.

To be honest, I was moved by what Simon had to say. He seemed so sad about his life, which from my perspective seemed so glamorous. I really wanted to hug him, but what had happened before between us stopped me, I guess. I told him that I was sure that everything would work out for him, that I hoped it would. He smiled at me in sort of a sad way and said he hoped so, too. And that was that. He then changed the topic of the conversation back to the NCW case.

That night was the beginning of a different relationship between Simon Clark and me. Although he didn't attempt anything physical, at the end of long days both on the road and in Nita City, we would often have long talks about the most personal of things. We were not intimate sexually, but we were intimate. He told me all about himself and his life and I did likewise. We spent an enormous amount of time together through the conclusion of the NCW case which was in early June of YR-3, when the case settled on very favorable terms for our client. The case was also a personal success. I was uniformly praised for my work on the case, in particular for my work on a protective order concerning some trade secrets of NCW's that was eventually granted by the court. I received a copy of a letter from the Vice President and General Counsel of NCW to Simon that acknowledged my contributions to the case. (SEE EXHIBIT 6)

NCW was so pleased with the outcome that they gave the members of the litigation team a trip, with spouses, for a week in the Bahamas. Everyone on the team including all the lawyers and the three paralegals were invited. Because I wasn't married and because Simon apparently never went anywhere with his wife, we were the only people there without a significant other. On our third night there, one thing led to another and Simon and I ended up sleeping together. I should have known that it was the wrong thing to do, but it happened anyway. We spent a terrific week together and Simon started talking about our future together.

I know that sometime during the week I asked Simon about when his son was going to graduate from high school and he told me that the boy needed to attend summer school in order to finish his degree and that he had pulled some strings to get him into college. Simon then volunteered that as soon as his boy was firmly in school that he was going to file for divorce. I know I should have recognized that he was repeating the pattern I heard he had with other women but I wanted our relationship to work. It was, after all, the only other serious relationship I had with a man other than my husband. I rationalized that this time Simon was really different for a number of reasons. First, unlike his other conquests I was not young. At that time I was in my late thirties and the other women were all in their twenties. Second, the way our relationship came about seemed so natural that I was sure he was sincere. Third, the rumors about Simon had lessened in recent years and I guess I wanted to believe that he had changed. Finally, the last kid being out of the house seemed like a good time to end a bad relationship, and from everything he said, he truly had a bad relationship with his wife.

The rest of that summer flew by. I was extremely happy with both my job and my personal life. My kids were doing great. They had met Simon and they seemed to like him. I didn't think that they knew what my relationship with him was, but as it turned out, they knew exactly what was going on. I told Simon that in light of my personal relationship with him, that I thought that I shouldn't work with him unless he absolutely needed me and he agreed. That summer I got terrific assignments, better than ever before. The cases were interesting and I was asked to work on interesting issues. My relationship with Simon was also terrific. We spent time away from the office together, including some weekend getaways. The only problem I had was on Labor Day weekend when he said that he had to spend it with his wife's family at some gathering in Martha's Vineyard. Simon told me that he really didn't want to go, but that it was the last chance he had to be with his son before he went off to school and that his other kids would also be there, including his oldest daughter who had just had her first child, a son. So even though I wasn't happy about it, I didn't put up a fuss about his going. I spent the weekend with my kids and as it turned out, we had a wonderful time.

I had my sixth-year evaluation right after Labor Day in YR-3. It was again held in Simon's office and Cliff Fuller was also there. I was thrilled when Simon told me that my grade for the year was an A. He said that the partners in the litigation section were very impressed with all the terrific work I did on the NCW case and with the enormous number of hours I billed for the year. I was also told that the management people at NCW were pleased with my work and that they would be pleased to have me work on other cases for them, which was consistent with the letter I had seen from NCW to Simon. (SEE EXHIBIT 6) Finally they told me that in my class, only one other person was graded at the A level, and that it looked very good for me for a positive partnership vote in the spring of YR-2. I was on cloud nine. Simon came out of his chair and gave me a big hug and a kiss. Because Cliff was in the room I was a little embarrassed, but at the time, nothing could have upset me. I do remember telling Simon that in the future we should not have any public displays of affection in the office, that I thought it was unprofessional and that others might hold it against me. Simon agreed with me, but said that at some point that the people in the firm would have to get used to it.

In fact, the day after my evaluation Cliff Fuller came to my office and asked if I minded a little advice from an old friend. I, of course, was interested in what he had to say. Cliff asked if I was aware of Simon's sexual history with women in the firm. I told him that I was, but that Simon had told me that once his son was away at college that he was going to leave his wife. When Cliff started to say something like, "he's said that before" I told him that I didn't want to talk about my relationship with Simon. Cliff backed off, but did say that he hoped things worked out for me, but if they didn't he wasn't sure that he could protect me at the firm. His statement sort of shook me, but I didn't respond. I felt that I had weathered the storm at the firm by way of long hours and hard work, and that was all the protection I needed. I'll have to admit that what Cliff said was unsettling and made me feel somewhat vulnerable, but I certainly didn't realize how vulnerable I turned out to be.

In September of YR-3 I started work on another case for NCW. It wasn't of the same size in dollar terms or complexity, but it was nonetheless interesting. Cliff Fuller was the partner in charge of the case, although Simon retained some supervisory control over all of NCW's litigation. As a result, when I had to travel to some of NCW's offices out of state, Simon, who was not involved in any special case at the time, sometimes came along. It was on one of these trips in late September or early October, that I had a conversation with Simon about his marital status. When I asked whether he had seen a lawyer about his divorce, his first response was to get angry and snapped out something like "the marriage lasted over twenty-five years, it takes some time to end it," but then he calmed down almost immediately and said that it was important for his son to be into his school routine before hitting him with that kind of news. He said that he wanted to give him a semester to get adjusted. I appreciated that his son had some academic problems in high school, and that college took some adjustment so I just accepted Simon's explanation.

I then got heavily involved in the NCW case and was working fairly hard on it with Cliff. Cliff never asked directly about my relationship with Simon, but every once in a while he asked how things were going for me. Even though by late fall I was having more questions about whether Simon would ever leave his wife, I never said anything about it to Cliff.

As it turned out, the Christmas holidays spelled the end of my relationship with Simon Clark. We got into a fight in early December about where Simon was going to spend Christmas day. He wanted to spend Christmas and the week after Christmas on a vacation with his family, including his wife, his children, and their families at his home in Palm Beach, Florida. He told me it was one of the only times when he got to see kids and even though he preferred to be with me, that he thought he should spend one last holiday with his family before his divorce. I was very unhappy about his holiday plans, but Simon promised me that at the end of the vacation, he would spend an extra day in Florida with his wife, and tell her that he was getting a divorce. This made me feel better, but of course he never did ask for the divorce.

Simon returned to Nita City right after the first of the year and came over to my house to see me. Fortunately my kids were out, because when I asked him how his wife took the divorce news, Simon told me that he hadn't said anything to her about the divorce. I got very angry and started screaming at him. He tried to calm me down and eventually did, and told me that he was still going to ask for the divorce, but that his son was having a rough time adjusting to school and that he wanted to wait until the boy had finished his freshman year before subjecting him to the upheaval of a divorce. I wanted to believe Simon, but I was still very angry. I told him to leave, which he did.

Over the next week, Simon was out of town on business. He called a number of times and sent flowers, but I didn't return his calls. I spent most of the week trying to figure out what I was going to do and came to the conclusion that even though I wanted him to, that Simon was probably never going to leave his wife. I decided to give him one last chance. When he returned to Nita City I invited him to my house for dinner. This would have been around January 15. I told him how I felt and that if he loved me and wanted to be with me that he had to get a lawyer and get divorce proceedings started in one week. He started to protest about his son, and I told him that I didn't want to hear about his son, that it was time for Simon to decide what he really wanted. I then sent him home and told him to call me with his decision.

The next week went by extremely slowly. The stress must have shown on me because a number of people asked me if I was well. That weekend Simon came to my house. He asked if I wanted to go away with him for a vacation in the Bahamas and pulled out some plane tickets from his pocket. I assumed he had told his wife he wanted a divorce, so I ran to hug him. I then asked him how she took the news and Simon told me to take it easy, but that it hadn't happened yet. I pushed him away and asked him to leave. He tried to grab me but when I insisted he just got angry. I'll never forget the anger on his face as he turned to walk out the door. As he left he said, "You're all the same. You don't realize when you've got a good thing going. You'll regret this, I promise you."

That's the last conversation I had with Simon Clark for about two months. He went off to try a case in Seattle. He never wrote or called. Apparently our breakup didn't affect him much because he won the case. When he returned to Nita City he did call to ask me to dinner, but I refused. I had spent the time he was away trying to get over Simon, and didn't want to take the chance of getting involved with him again. That two months had been very hard for me. I had trouble at work concentrating in the beginning, but eventually I came around and emersed myself in my work. But probably because I wasn't eating particularly well, I caught a lot of colds, some of which were bad enough to keep me out of work. They continued well into the spring of YR-2.

Because of my health, I welcomed the fact that my assignments seemed to lighten up in the winter and early spring of YR-2, and I wasn't very busy. As it turned out, that was only a portent of things to come. In May of YR-2, Cliff Fuller asked me to come to his office.

Q: I assume you went to Mr. Fuller's office.

A: Yes I did.

Q: What did he have to say?

A: He told me that the firm was about to consider three people in my class for partnership and that if I wanted, I too could be brought up.

Q: Was that it?

A: No, he said, however, that given the drop-off in my production and the lingering problems some people had with my law school background, my early refusal to travel, and my lack of toughness, that it was his advice that I put off the partnership decision for another year so I could improve my chances.

Q: How did you respond?

A: When I protested, he told me that he was only the messenger, that he was in my corner and that I could count on his vote, but that he was fairly certain that if I pushed the matter, I would be turned down.

Q: What did you say?

A: I asked Cliff whether this was Simon's doing, and he deflected my question and told me that this was his best advice, but that he was willing to fight for me if that was my desire. He told me to think it over for a couple of days and get back to him.

The next couple of days I went through all the options in my head. It became obvious that Simon was doing to me what he apparently had done to his other former lovers. I then realized that the drop off in my assignments was no accident, and that while I was feeling fortunate to have some break in my assignments, that the lack of assignments was designed to hurt me. No, I didn't protest the lack of work to anyone. I just viewed it as a cyclical thing. I had been very busy in the fall, working on the second NCW case with Cliff and several other matters. My billables for September, YR-3 through January, YR-2 were approximately 850 hours, which on average was better than my previous year. After speaking with Cliff, I checked my billables for February, YR-2 through May, YR-2 and they were only 550 hours. I'll admit that wasn't very good, but if you projected from the first four months together with the second four months, to the last four months of the year, I would have ended up with a respectable 2,100 hours for the year. That is, I billed 1,400 hours for the first two-thirds of the year, which projects to 2,100 hours for the entire year, assuming I got decent assignments. I eventually concluded that I was better off coming up for partnership in that year, while my NCW success was still fresh in everyone's mind, than waiting for a year of reduced assignments and letting them drive me out that way. I gave Cliff my decision, and although he tried to talk me out of it, he promised to go forward.

About a week later, Cliff came to my office and gave me the bad news. He said that I didn't make it out of the litigation section with a recommendation of partnership. He said that it was close, but that I had just missed. He told me that the firm was giving me six months to find another position. I was obviously very upset. I asked Cliff if Simon spoke in favor of me. Cliff said that the meeting was confidential and that he couldn't tell me who said what. He did say that he was sure that Simon would give me a good reference if I wanted one. He then said he was sorry. I also asked Cliff how the three others who were up for partnership had fared. He told me two men, Roger Kramer and Mark Hancock, had made partner, and that Michael DeAngelo had decided to put off consideration for partnership a year. I asked Cliff if I could come up again in the next year, and he told me that once an associate chose to go forward, as I did, there was no turning back. He also said that he doubted that a new vote would make any difference.

I was hurt and angry over my treatment by P & G and was convinced that the cause of my being denied a partnership was because of my dumping Simon Clark. I therefore went to the Nita office of the Equal Employment Opportunity Commission to file a complaint. After some research, I learned that complaining to the EEOC was a necessary prerequisite to bringing suit against P & G. The interviewer seemed sympathetic, but said that it was unlikely that she would get to my claim for a long while. She told me to contact her in 180 days so that she could issue a "Right to Sue" letter if I wanted to pursue my claim in the courts. I did so, and received a form giving me the right to sue in December of YR-2, shortly after I resigned from P & G.

I took some time off from work to sort through my career options. During this period, I quietly looked into some other associate positions, but nothing really caught my fancy, and although I sent out some resumes, nothing came of it. Several firms seemed to be interested initially and had me send reference letters, but only a couple of firms gave me what I would consider a full interview, and no job offer was made. Because I didn't have the ability to bring any business to a new firm at that time, my prospects in Nita City to be a partner in a large firm didn't seem great. What did surprise me, was that I didn't even receive any permanent associate offers. I thought too about moving to another city, but Nita had been my home and I really didn't want to leave.

One night as I was absent mindedly going through the mail, I saw an alumni newsletter from the law school and I started to think about teaching as a career. The next day I called Gary Sherman, who was in my associates class at P & G and who had left for a teaching career several years before. He was very helpful and enthusiastic about my trying to find a teaching job. He advised me that the best thing I could do was to work some interesting project from my practice into a law review article and attempt to get published before the law school hiring convention in the fall of YR-2.

The more I thought of it, the more teaching appealed to me. During my law school years I had enjoyed the research and writing experience that I had with the *Law Review*, and I remember harboring some thoughts about a teaching career sometime in the future when my kids were grown and I only had myself to look after. In practice, you never get to finish looking into some of the interesting legal and intellectual issues that arise beyond what is necessary to deal with a client's problems and that was always somewhat frustrating to me. In addition, although my kids were still in school, and the money that you can make in practice was still important, I had never acquired a life style that demanded a huge salary so even though I realized that I would have to take a substantial pay cut, I thought that I should explore the teaching option. It was early in my career for such a move, but I thought that exploration of the teaching option was worth the effort.

I went back to the firm the next week and started to look back over my files for some of the issues that had intrigued me when I was working on them, but never got finished, at least to my satisfaction. When I was working on a case, I would often make some notes about how I would like to explore a particular issue in the future if time allowed. Within a week I identified two particularly interesting issues and started looking into them. I ended up writing on the tension between the law of privilege and work product, when such material is used by a client for the purposes of refreshing recollection, and the right of opposing counsel to see such material. Given that I was assigned very little work, there was little to distract me from my scholarly work, and by the early fall, I had an article to be submitted for publication. Working on the article was one of the most satisfying intellectual experiences of my career and confirmed that I should continue to explore a position in legal education. I was lucky in that an article that had been promised for a symposium issue on current issues in litigation in the Nita University Law Review did not materialize and my article was accepted to fill that void.

I spent the rest of the fall working on another article between the sporadic assignments I received from the firm, and this piece on conflicts of interest in antitrust litigation was in rough draft form by the time of the Association of American Law Schools hiring convention. I got about ten initial interviews and was invited to four on-campus interviews in December of YR-2. As a result of the interviewing process, I received an offer from Conwell University School of Law. Fortunately for me, the offer did not come through until the later spring of YR-1. At the same time, I was working as an Adjunct Professor at my alma mater, filling in for Professor Levinson, who was visiting at another law school. When Professor Levinson decided to stay at that school, I received an offer from Nita University to join the faculty as an Associate Professor in the fall of YR-1. I am told that the offer was based in part on strong reports on my teaching from the students in my spring YR-1 classes. Because Nita City is my home, I chose to take the offer from Nita University, even though I'm sure I would have enjoyed working with Gary Sherman at Conwell Law School. My starting salary at the Law School was $75,000.

The law school offers came at a good time for me because I needed an ego boost and two teaching offers in a tough market restored some of the self-esteem I lost in my unsuccessful search for practice jobs in Nita City. As I said, I had applied to a number of law firms, beginning in the summer of YR-2, but no positions came open for me. I had a number of interviews, but received no offers. Initially, I thought that the whole experience at P & G had demoralized me, and that I was not coming across as very confident in the interviews I had, or that my foray into academic writing had steered me towards an academic career, which had some impact on my enthusiasm in law firm job interviews. As it turned out, my real problem with law firm jobs was apparently Simon Clark.

Cliff Fuller told me in June of YR-2 that he had written a glowing recommendation concerning my abilities for Simon Clark's signature, and that I should feel free to use both him and Simon as references when looking for a law firm position. Although I was hesitant to use Simon as a reference, I did so after Cliff showed me a copy of the letter he drafted for Simon's signature. (SEE EXHIBIT 10) I got a phone call after the first of the year in YR-1 from a friend of mine at Morrison & Farrow, which is a law firm in Nita City to which I had applied in June or July of YR-2. This friend told me that she had seen the Simon Clark recommendation letter and that it was not a good one. She also told me that John Randall of her firm spoke with Simon about me, and that Simon was very negative in his evaluation of my abilities. She eventually made a copy of Simon's letter from their files which obviously is not a good letter of recommendation, and not consistent with my performance at P & G. (SEE EXHIBIT 11) I recognize the handwriting at the bottom of the page on Exhibit 11, that says to "be careful," as Simon Clark's. He obviously deep-sixed me with Morrison & Farrow. I can only assume that he did the same with other firms who inquired of him, which explains why I received no law firm job offers.

I stayed on at P & G until the end of my six-month grace period, just to save some more money. I turned in my resignation to Cliff Fuller. Cliff has been very supportive of me in my searching for positions, both in practice and academia, and although he tried to get excited about the adjunct position, I could tell he was disappointed for me. He inquired about my finances and offered to loan me some money if I needed it. I told him that I appreciated his concern, but that I would be all right. I had cashed in my retirement account at P & G, so that more than covered me for the short term when combined with my salary as an adjunct at the law school. I was also hopeful that one of my law school teaching interviews would pan out into a full-time position. Apparently P & G was notified by the EEOC about my complaint against them, because Cliff offered to give whatever testimony he could about my time at P & G. Since my resignation from the firm, I have had dinner with Cliff on a number of occasions. He has been a good friend to me. We don't often talk about P & G, but Cliff did tell me late YR-2 or early YR-1 that he had become disenchanted with the firm and firm politics.

In January of YR-1, when I told Cliff what Simon had done to me when I had applied for law firm jobs, he was visibly upset. He later checked and found that Simon had indeed written his own reference letter which was far from complimentary to all of the firms I applied to and informed them that Simon would act as a reference. It was when Cliff called me with that news that he also told me that he was considering leaving the firm for a position with NCW. In the end, Cliff was appointed the Vice President and General Counsel of Nita Computer World. He started with them in April of YR-1. Shortly after beginning at NCW, Cliff and I had one of our dinners. At that time he offered me a position in NCW's legal department to assist in managing the company's litigation. Although I was flattered by the offer, I had just been offered the full-time position at the law school and had accepted that offer. Even though the NCW job would have paid a starting salary of $90,000, and my law school salary started at $75,000, I wanted to give teaching a good try. My semester as an adjunct had been very challenging and rewarding, and, as I said, I was well received by my students. I also liked the fact that research and writing whatever I was interested in was a job requirement.

Although I am very happy at the law school, I do miss the different challenges and the highs and lows of practice. I worked very hard at P & G to succeed and deserved to be treated better that I was. I believe that my failure to receive an offer of partnership was a direct result of my breaking off my relationship with Simon Clark. I also believe that P & G discriminates against women. No woman has ever been made a partner in the litigation section to perform regular commercial litigation while I was there. The only women partners in litigation were either Jayne Post's domestic relations group, where in addition to Jayne there are three other women partners (Sherry Barker, Ann Feinman, and Georgia Bratton) and in the bankruptcy group which has only three partners, two of whom are women (Cheryl Stein and Kathryn Kowalski). Of the general litigation partners, of which there are thirty in the firm, there are no women.

I also believe that Simon Clark slandered me when talking to people at firms where I applied for associate positions after being forced out of P & G. Although his letter (SEE EXHIBIT 11) is not negative in an absolute sense, it is not a fair representation of my work at the firm, and certainly is not the kind of letter on which you base a positive hiring decision. In addition, his oral statements, at least to John Randall at Morrison & Farrow, (SEE EXHIBIT 18) were out-and-out false.

STATEMENT OF CLIFFORD FULLER

My name is Cliff Fuller. I am forty-three years old and work as the Vice President and General Counsel of Nita Computer World, which is a national wholesaler and retailer of computers and other electronic equipment. Until April 1st of YR-1, I was a general litigation partner at the law firm of Parker & Gould (P & G) in Nita City. For the period YR-4 until the time that I left the firm, I was the deputy chair of the litigation section of the firm. I am single, having gotten a divorce from my wife, Gerry, in YR-14. Fortunately, we did not have any children.

I was born and raised in Nita City and graduated from the public schools. I have six siblings, all but two of whom still live in the area. My brother Mike lives in Los Angeles and my sister, Carol, lives in Atlanta. My parents, both of whom are still living, also live in Nita City. My father is a retired postal worker. I received my undergraduate degree in Political Science from Bucknell University in Lewisburg, Pennsylvania, in YR-20 where I was an academic scholarship student. I graduated with honors, and although I was accepted by a number of the so-called top law schools, none of them offered me any substantial financial aid, so when I was accepted to the University of Nita School of Law I decided to take advantage of the relatively low in-state tuition and enrolled in September of YR-20. I was also married in the summer of YR-20 to Gerry. She was also a graduate of Bucknell, which is where we met.

While I was going to law school, Gerry attended the business school at Nita University. She got her MBA in YR-18. Gerry's job opportunities were somewhat limited by the fact that I still had a year to go at law school. Although I considered transferring to another school, wherever Gerry's best job opportunities took us, I was elected the editor-in-chief of the Law Review, and we thought that it was important for my career that I finish up at Nita University. Gerry turned down some very attractive offers elsewhere, and took a job in Nita City. As it turned out, I always felt guilty about that decision, and I think that Gerry was always a little resentful. This was especially so when I received an offer from P & G which was then, and I think now, considered to be one of the best firms in the region. I think that Gerry felt, and I think it was fair for her to feel, that she had sacrificed in her career for me, while I never had to sacrifice anything in my career for her. This resentment was really the foundation of our marital problems which persisted over the years until we separated in YR-15 and eventually divorced in YR-14. Gerry now lives and works in New York City, where she is a very successful investment counselor.

To be honest, I was surprised that I ended up at P & G. Although I had a good record at law school, graduating first in my class, P & G had the reputation of being an elitist law firm and I was the first Nita law graduate to ever receive an offer from them. Even though I had offers from

POLISI DEPOSITION MATERIALS

most of the other large law firms in the city for the summer between my second and third year, I chose to go to P & G to prove to them that Nita was actually a fine law school. Perhaps because of that, I worked especially hard, and apparently made a good impression, because I was offered a position as an associate with the firm in YR-17, which I accepted. Aside from the honor of being the first Nita law grad, the other reason I accepted P & G's offer was Simon Clark.

During my summer at P & G, I was assigned to work with Simon Clark on a fairly routine contract action involving two Nita City companies. He gave me interesting work to do, and always took the time to explain how what I was doing fit into the whole of the case. He also invited me along on depositions and to settlement negotiations. I was allowed to sit in on planning and strategy sessions as well. I found the whole experience fascinating, so when Simon was complimentary about my work and urged me to come on board at P & G, my decision was made.

As it turned out, Simon Clark became my mentor at the firm. He made sure that I got the right assignments and avoided the political pitfalls that exist in every law firm. He also took a special interest in my work and development. Whenever Simon was involved in a big case he requested that I be assigned to work with him. Because I had no family responsibilities I was always available to travel on the firm's business. While I was an associate, Simon became recognized as one of the leading litigators in the firm. Much because of Simon's guidance, I was fast-tracked to a partnership and was made a partner in the firm in YR-11, a year before anyone else in my class of associates, and a year before the earliest partnership decisions at P & G are normally made. I believe that Simon was not only responsible for training me and getting me good work to do, but also that he was the driving force in my being made a partner, at least on the fast-track basis.

While Simon Clark is a role model for me as a lawyer, he does have his Achilles' heel. Although he is married with four children, Simon is well known in the firm for having extramarital affairs with young women in the office. This was especially so in my early years at the firm. It seemed that every few months another rumor would circulate about another affair with either a paralegal or an associate. I don't have much specific information, but I do know of several instances when I was either approached by the young woman involved or where the affair was public.

One such public affair was with a paralegal by the name of Ellen Dorsen. She and Simon had a relationship that lasted some six months or so, during YR-12 and maybe carrying over into YR-11. Ms. Dorsen was quite public about the relationship and spoke openly about how she and

Simon were doing this or that together. I also overheard her say that Simon was going to leave his wife to marry her. According to the rumor mill, that was Simon's normal *modus operandi*: To promise that he would get a divorce, and then fail to go through with the promise, which usually led to the end of the relationship. I am aware that at some point Simon and Ms. Dorsen broke up, because she was working on a case with me at the time, and I had to ask that she be removed from the case because her work suddenly became very sloppy, which was not the norm for her. I believe that her work never came back to normal and that the firm eventually had to let her go.

I am also personally aware of two affairs that Simon had with young women associates. I know that he was involved, for a brief time in YR-11, with Karen Newman, who was a fourth-year associate with the firm. Karen was well regarded in the firm, but generally not considered partnership material. In the normal course of things, I expect she would have left the firm within a year of when she did, but I suspect, now, that her affair with Simon Clark hastened her leaving. She and Simon worked briefly together on a case that took them to Dallas with some frequency. Because I was not involved in that case I only became aware of their sexual relationship after the fact when Karen approached me to get some advice.

She told me that she had a brief affair with Simon Clark, but broke it off when it became obvious to her that he had no intention of leaving his wife. She complained to me that her work assignments had dropped off both in terms of quantity (she was having a hard time keeping her billable hours up) and quality (she was assigned to work on several domestic relations matters, which were not considered quality work within the firm) and that she was afraid that she was being sabotaged by Simon Clark. She said she was coming to me because of my relationship with Simon, which was public knowledge. I did not believe that Simon would do such a thing, and I told her so. I did counsel her about her career and when she told me that she felt that she had no realistic opportunity to make partner at P & G, I suggested that a fourth-year associate had very marketable skills and that she should consider moving earlier as opposed to later. I assured her that I could write a letter on her behalf and that I would ask Simon to do so as well. When I asked Simon to write a recommendation for Karen, he told me to draft something for his signature and that he would be glad to help. Shortly thereafter Karen left the firm for a position with another firm in Nita City.

The only other relationship between Simon and an associate that I have some firsthand knowledge about, other than with Maggie Polisi, was with Carol Merritt. Carol was assigned to one of Simon's cases in YR-10 on which I was acting as second chair. The case involved some paper mills in Washington state and a lawsuit by an environmentalist group to halt the harvesting of substantial forests. We spent quite a bit of time in YR-10 taking discovery and in motion practice in Washington. Carol was a fourth-year associate and was one of two associates assigned to follow up on discovery and essentially manage the case as it proceeded. Although she was married and the case took her away from home for at least four days of every week, she seemed to enjoy the work and did a quite good job.

Sometime during the early stages of the case, Simon and Carol began a relationship. They were circumspect in the beginning, but as time went on became quite public about their relationship, at least while they were in Washington. I never saw them together in Nita City. The relationship was serious enough that at some point Carol left her husband. The affair between Carol and Simon lasted about as long as the case, and when the case ended in late YR-10, the relationship ended shortly thereafter. Carol took it quite hard, and took about a month's leave from the firm. I know that Simon felt bad about the situation because he called me into his office and explained that Carol had decided not to rejoin the firm. He said he regretted what had happened between them, but that it was just one of those things. He then told me that Carol was back with her husband and that they were moving to Washington, D.C. He asked me to write some glowing recommendations for her, based on her work in the Washington case (which was actually quite good) and send them to a list of his friends in various firms in D.C. I also wrote to some friends of mine and within a few months Carol had joined up with a very good firm in D.C. I believe that she's a partner there now and doing quite well.

Other than his affair with Maggie Polisi, I have no other specific information about Simon Clark's alleged extramarital activity. In fact, in the years before his relationship with Maggie, I heard very few, if any, rumors about him, but given my relationship with Simon, I don't think that people would consider me a good person with whom to share such gossip. On the other hand, we do work together from time to time and if Simon had a serious affair, especially with someone in the firm, I think I would have heard about it. But P & G is a big firm, so I can't be sure. I know that in YR-7 Simon's son was in a bad car accident that seriously threatened his life. Simon's concern for his son and the attendant family crisis might also have straightened him out for a while.

P & G has approximately 330 lawyers, who practice in four sections. The litigation section is the largest with approximately 160 lawyers, less than a third of whom are partners. Within the litigation section, most lawyers work in general commercial litigation. We have a small subgroup that does domestic relations work and another small subgroup that does bankruptcy litigation. The corporate section has approximately 110 lawyers, with the same partner-associate ratio as the litigation section. The tax section has about thirty-five lawyers, about 60 percent of whom are partners. The estate section has approximately twenty lawyers, most of whom are partners.

As I said earlier, I was the deputy chair of the litigation section of the firm for the almost four years. Simon Clark was the chair for three of those four years. The deputy chair is chosen by the chair, so I started as deputy solely at the discretion of Simon Clark. Our main functions were to oversee client-firm relations and to evaluate the performance of the lawyers in our section of the firm, in particular the associates as they progressed from hiring to partnership. When Simon stepped down as chair in September of YR-2, I continued to work as the deputy under the current chair, Rob Bryant, until I left the firm in April of YR-1.

The partnership decision at P & G is based on a series of evaluations of the performance of associates during their time with the firm. I can only speak with specificity about the litigation section of the firm as to how an associate moves from hiring to an offer of partnership. The firm normally hires twenty associates for the litigation section. The normal partnership track is seven to nine years. In the history of the firm, there are two people, myself and Alice Abraham in the tax section of the firm, who have been made partners in six years. By the time that the partnership decision is made, only three or four people from the beginning associates class are considered for partnership. At least 75 percent of the associates who come forward for a partnership decision are successful. The rest of the associates from each class leave the firm to other positions, or are retained by the firm as permanent associates.

Each associate's performance is evaluated every year, as close in time to the associate's anniversary date as possible. Typically, because most associates begin work in the fall, most evaluations are in September or October. Our system is fairly simple. About a month before the evaluation is to take place, the chair and deputy chair of the litigation section identify from time records the partners for whom the associate has worked during the previous year. Each of those partners are briefly interviewed and asked to evaluate the performance of the associate and to provide any comments on how the associate's performance can improve. The rest of the partnership is also generally solicited to provide any comments they have on any associate. We also consider the number of billable hours the associate has worked. As the partnership decision gets closer the ability of the associate to attract and/or maintain business is also an important factor. The chairman and the deputy then amalgamate all the information and assign a grade of A–F to the associate's performance for the year. That amalgamation is kept in a series of memos written by the chair of the section, or the deputy, to the file of each associate as they progress through the firm. Exhibits 3A–3G are the evaluation memos for Maggie Polisi. Exhibits 5A–5H are the evaluation memos for Mike DeAngelo, although I did not participate in his evaluation for YR-1 which took place after I left the firm. The associates are not shown the evaluation memo, but they do receive a letter each year which shows their raise in salary which is tied to the evaluation. Exhibits 4A–4F are Maggie Polisi's salary letters for her time with the firm.

The A grade is reserved for the most extraordinary of performances, and is generally not awarded until an associate's fifth or sixth year. It is a clear indication that the associate is likely to be offered a partnership sometime in the future. The B grade is, as it usually works out, the best grade associates can receive in their first four years with the firm. It is a sign that the associate is performing very well and is making good progress towards partnership, although partnership is not mentioned in evaluations until the fifth year. Only about three to five members of each associates class receive B grades in their first through fourth years. The B grade in the fifth year and beyond is still considered excellent, but generally connotes that the associate is borderline for partnership. An associate will typically receive at least one grade of A before they are considered for partnership, and most typically in the year in which they come up for partnership.

The C grade is the typical grade received in the first two years of an associate's career. It reflects a good, but not exemplary, performance. The C grade in years three and four, is usually a good indicator that the associate will not be made a partner and associates with a C grade in his or her fourth year are typically advised that it would be appropriate for them to seek other employment. In some cases, an associate will be particularly bright and do very well in analysis of legal issues, but fail to have the necessary communication and advocacy skills to become a litigation partner in the firm. In those cases, the associate may be approached with an offer as a permanent associate. Permanent associates have no possibility of being made partners and are salaried employees of the firm paid at approximately the same level as a sixth-year associate on the partnership track. A grade of C in the fifth year is usually a clear sign that the associate will not make partner. With some of these associates, the firm will make efforts to place them in general counsel offices of our good clients. Those positions pay very well and usually have excellent benefits. It is the firm's interest to place former associates with clients in that it fosters good client relations. In fact, I have several former P & G associates working for me at NCW in the General Counsel's office.

The D grade is given for below expectation performance. While it is possible for an associate to have a D grade in the first year and improve and eventually go on to partnership, a D in the first two years will usually result in a recommendation to seek other employment. A grade of D in each of the first three years results in the setting of a termination date, usually thirty days after the evaluation.

The F grade is reserved for situations where the associate has performed in an incompetent manner. Because we are very careful in our hiring decisions, I know of no associate who has ever received an F grade in an evaluation.

Once the grade has been assigned, the chair of the section, the deputy chair of the section, and the associate meet for the purpose of the evaluation. The associate is first given his or her grade for the year and then is given an explanation of the basis for the grade. The source of individual partner comments is not divulged to the associate, but the nature of the comment often serves to identify its source. During the meeting the section chair will read the amalgamation of the comments that have been prepared by the chair and the deputy chair. If questions are asked, the chair may refer to notes from interviews with individual partners, but that is not the norm. The associate is then given an opportunity to comment on the evaluation or ask questions. The associate is then told their raise for the next year. The associate does not receive any written evaluation. The only record that is kept is the amalgamation of the comments from the partners and the records on billable hours. Individual interview notes are destroyed after the evaluation meeting. In addition, once an associate is made a partner, the only records that are maintained are those of the grades assigned for each year and their billable hours for each year. Once an associate leaves the firm, the records of grades and billable hours are kept for approximately five or six years, in case the firm is contacted for a letter of recommendation for another position. The evaluation memos are destroyed once the associate leaves the firm. Exhibits 7A and 7B are a compilation of the records concerning the class of associates at P & G who began as associates in YR-9. It shows the billable hours and grades for each associate in that class during their time at P & G.

While the associate does not get a copy of the evaluation record, they do receive, as I said earlier, a written confirmation of their raise. Raises are based on a set formula, that coincides with the grade that the associate has received. The raise scale is as follows: A–7 percent; B–5 percent; C–3 percent; and D–2 percent. Salaries are also adjusted periodically to reflect increases in base salary. These increases are irrespective of merit and are reflected on the salary letters as market adjustments.

Partnership decisions are usually made in June of the seventh year of an associate's tenure with the firm. In order for an associate to be made a partner, the associate must be nominated by the partners in their section. The nomination is by majority vote. That nomination goes to the Executive Committee of the firm. The Executive Committee then recommends the associate to the entire partnership. The Executive Committee normally implements the recommendations of the four sections of the firm (litigation, corporate, tax and estates) unless in the committee's opinion the particular section is too top-heavy with partners. During my time at the firm, I know of no occasion when the Executive Committee has not recommended for partnership an associate who has been nominated by his or her section, although I believe there was one circumstance where an associate was made to wait a year by the Executive Committee before they were recommended to the entire partnership. The recommendation of the executive committee is then voted on by all partners. A majority vote is required to achieve partnership. It is very unusual for the entire partnership to vote down an associate who has been recommended by both his or her section and the Executive Committee. In my time at P & G that has only happened twice.

I first met Maggie Polisi when she came to work as a paralegal at the firm at about the same time that I started as an associate. I didn't have very much to do with her until YR-15 when she was assigned to work one of Simon Clark's cases to which I was also assigned. This case, involving a dispute among the largest banks in the state of Nita, was extremely complex and involved difficult legal issues. It was the case in which Simon Clark established himself as one of the best, if not the best, litigators and trial lawyers in the firm, and probably in the city as well. Maggie was chosen to work as one of the trial paralegals when the case came to trial in January of YR-13. As a fourth-year associate, I was assigned to coordinate between the two partners who were trying the case and the paralegals. During that trial, Maggie and I got to work quite closely together, and I was very impressed with her intellect and how quickly she was able to assimilate and understand directions given to her, and anticipate other needs in the trial. Simon Clark was also impressed with Maggie's work and I know that he encouraged her to apply to law school, which she did. Since she was applying to Nita University School of Law, as an alumni I volunteered to write a recommendation letter for her.

Maggie was accepted to Nita law school and attended the evening division. This was necessary because she was a single mother of small children and she needed to support them while she attended school. She continued to work as a paralegal at P & G during her first year of law school. As it turned out, she did very well in school and we offered her a position as a law clerk with the firm, which meant a pay raise for her. During her four years of law school, Maggie did quite a lot of work for me. She was bright, insightful, and talented. I remember that I called Simon's attention to her work from time to time and kept him posted on all of Maggie's success in law school. He was thoughtful enough to compliment her work as I did, but I know coming from Simon Clark, it meant more to her. As it turned out she graduated magna cum laude, finished first in her class and was an editor of the law review; all while working full time at P & G and having the responsibilities of a single mother.

As you can tell I was, and am, quite a fan of Maggie Polisi. In the early fall of her fourth and final year of law school, unbeknownst to her, I went to Simon Clark and spoke on Maggie's behalf about her getting a position as an associate with P & G. Although Simon didn't embrace the idea immediately, he thought it worth checking out with the hiring committee. P & G had never hired one of its law clerks as an associate, as a matter of policy, and had never hired a graduate of Nita Law School's evening division, I guess based on some misconception that the evening division is somehow different than the day division in quality of education. Not hiring law clerks made sense as a matter of policy in that it kept competition among the law clerks, which might have interfered with productivity, at a minimum. Not hiring graduates of the evening division of Nita Law School made no sense at all. At least at Nita University, the law curriculum is taught by the same instructors in the day and evening division and no distinction is made between the divisions. If anything, because the evening division students all have demanding day jobs, their accomplishments at law school are more commendable, not less.

Simon and I quietly circulated the idea around the hiring committee, of which I was a member and Simon was the chair, and most people on the committee seemed amenable to recruiting Maggie. Our job was made easier by the fact that the summer associates from the previous summer were less impressive than usual and that it looked that our yield of full-time associates from that group would be lower than usual.

We approached Maggie with the idea of applying to P & G and she seemed genuinely flattered. She did end up applying and going through the formal interviewing process. Maggie easily made it through the preliminary interviews and was invited to the firm for a full day of interviews. She apparently did quite well. Given that we already knew the high quality of her work, as supported by Simon Clark, who was known in the firm as being very demanding, in many ways Maggie was a much more certain product than someone who had only spent a summer with us, or someone who had never worked in the firm.

The only major stumbling block was Maggie's insistence, given her responsibilities as a single parent, that she not be assigned to any cases that took her our of Nita City for extended periods of time. Because P & G had and has a national practice, this requirement somewhat limited the range of matters on which Maggie could work, and this caused problems with several of my partners, the most vocal of whom was Jayne Post. This seemed odd in that Jayne worked exclusively on domestic relations matters, that were almost always local in nature, but her complaint did have some merit. Simon and I argued on Maggie's behalf, that there was plenty of work of varying complexity in and around Nita City, and that after all, the children would eventually grow up and leave the house. That argument seemed to carry the day. There were also some questions asked about the quality of the education in the evening division of Nita law school, but I was able to answer those questions sufficiently to remove that as an impediment.

The committee eventually voted to offer Maggie a position as an associate. Simon Clark made the offer personally and Maggie accepted. She later thanked me for all my help, and told me that she would prove that our confidence in her was deserved. Maggie did come to see me in July of YR-9 when she received the formal letter from the firm which set her salary. She was concerned that the language of the letter could be interpreted so that she could be required to travel extensively, despite the clear understanding that she had with the firm. (SEE EXHIBIT 2) I assured her that the firm was well aware of her special requirements and not to worry about the letter, that it was just a form letter.

I became a mentor of sorts for Maggie Polisi. I knew how important Simon's guidance had been for me as I worked myself up through the firm to partnership, and I thought that I could give Maggie similar guidance. I felt a special responsibility towards her because I had recruited her to the firm, and because she was a graduate of my law school. I knew that there could be added pressure on an associate who was the first from a particular school to work at the firm, or in her case, the first from the evening division of Nita U., because of how it felt for me when I was the first associate from the law school at P & G. In addition, I liked Maggie as a person, and admired the way that she had worked her way through law school, while at the same time having the responsibilities of being a single mother.

I also talked up Maggie among my partners so that they would request her to work on various projects. I was confident of Maggie's abilities, and with the right opportunities, I was sure that she would flourish at the firm. I also warned her to avoid being pigeonholed in less-desirable specialties within the firm. For example, within the litigation section of the firm, the vast majority of lawyers work in general commercial litigation which involves the full range of problems faced by our large corporate clients. There were, at the time that Maggie joined the firm, and there remain today, two small subgroups within the litigation section: a domestic relations group headed by Jayne Post and a bankruptcy group headed by John Crandall. These subgroups, because of their size and specialty, carried less clout than general litigation and it was, while I was with the firm, much harder to become a partner if an associate specialized in either of those groups than if they worked on general commercial litigation matters. First, the associate's work is exposed to a broader range of lawyers, and second, the work is thought of as having greater complexity and requiring higher analytical skills. These perceptions may have been inaccurate, but because they existed, they might as well have been real.

The domestic relations subgroup was a particularly bad choice for women associates because many of the older members of the firm viewed that practice with disdain, referring to it in a derogatory way as "women's work." Now that you ask, it's true that while I was with the firm, the only women partners in the litigation section were in those two areas.

I did my best to guide Maggie through the political minefields of the law firm, and she seemed grateful for my help. She also followed my advice most of the time, and through the first four years of her practice at P & G she did quite well. She was given good assignments, and impressed most of the partners for whom she worked. She worked for me on a number of cases in that period and did terrific work. There was some mild criticism of her writing in her first year, but that was typical of almost all of our associates. I believe she was graded at the C level in her first year, which put her in the top half of her associates class. I recall that she was upset with her evaluation, but I told her not to be, that the grade was typical and that she should just keep on doing good work and she would be fine.

In Maggie's second, third, and fourth years, she was graded at the B level, which I believe put her in the top three or four of her associates class. Her evaluations were uniformly good, and although I did help her get good assignments when I could, she was in demand by other partners as well. There were very few negative comments. A couple of the old-timers at the firm, would, from time to time, complain about her not being "aggressive" or "tough" enough, which I believe was a code for "she's a woman," but those comments should not have been taken seriously and I told Maggie as much. The one negative comment that had some substance came from Jayne Post, who felt that it was inappropriate for Maggie to confine her practice to cases that kept her in Nita City, or at least required minimum time out of town. Jayne felt that Maggie's lack of travel created a burden on other associates, and kept the firm from being able to evaluate how Maggie performed with the added stress of having to work in unfamiliar places, dealing with an unfamiliar bench and bar. She felt this evaluation was important because so much of P & G's practice was outside of Nita City, and if Maggie made partner she would be expected to travel where her cases took her. When I reminded Jayne that the travel issue had been raised, discussed, and decided when Maggie was interviewing with the firm, her response was that the children had to be old enough at that time to be able to deal with childcare help in the home when Maggie was required to travel.

Maggie had a terrible fifth year as an associate, and it could not have come at a worse time. By the time an associate is in her fifth year the partners take a very close look at her performance. This is because by this point the associate is fully trained and is dealing with relatively complex factual settings involving difficult analytical issues. As a result, the fifth year usually provides an excellent marker for partnership potential, Maggie's terrible year, however, was really not a reflection of abilities, but caused by a series of personal problems.

As I understand it, both of Maggie's children, who were teenagers at the time, went through difficult periods, while at the same time her father was diagnosed with cancer and died. The coincidence of these events kept Maggie from being focused on her work. Her billable hours dipped significantly, and quite frankly the quality of her work diminished as well. Because I was aware of her personal situation, I covered for her on the work she was doing for me, but other partners were less generous in evaluating her work product. This was even though they were aware of Maggie's personal problems. Their complaint was that at P & G the pressure of the practice and the need to perform at a high level does not diminish because a lawyer has personal problems. They expressed concern that a pattern of such behavior at the onset of personal crises would develop, and that was a problem. I was privy to all of these comments because by that time, in YR-4, Simon Clark was made the chair of the litigation section, and he asked me to be his deputy.

The end result of Maggie's evaluation was that she was graded at the C level for the year. The partners in the litigation section authorized Simon to use his influence to place her in the general counsel's office of one of our client companies, or agree to give her a strong recommendation should she choose to seek alternative employment herself. Some of the partners in the section felt that those should be Maggie's only two options. Mainly because of my faith in Maggie and her ability, and at my insistence, Simon persuaded the litigation partners that Maggie should be given a shot at redeeming herself by working on a very important antitrust case of his that was heating up for one of our best clients, Nita Computer World (NCW). If it had not been for Simon Clark, Maggie's career with P & G would have ended in YR-4. That's why what happened to Maggie later on was so ironic.

Simon and I presented Maggie with her evaluation and with the options available to her. Although she was disappointed with her grade, she opted to work on the NCW litigation, as I knew she would. No one can doubt the heart of Maggie Polisi.

I was not involved in the NCW antitrust case, but I got periodic reports from Simon on Maggie's performance. As I predicted, she performed magnificently, according to Simon, and he complimented me on my judgment. Around the end of YR-4 or the beginning of YR-3, I had a conversation with Simon Clark about Maggie Polisi. He confirmed that she was still doing a great job, but that he was interested in finding out what I knew about Maggie's personal life. I told him about her children, but I knew that he was aware of them and the problems Maggie had with them the previous year. He asked whether I knew if she was involved with anyone romantically, and I answered honestly that I didn't know. It was obvious that Simon's interest in Maggie went beyond the professional.

For some reason I felt very protective towards Maggie, and told Simon that if he was interested in her, other than as a lawyer, that he had better be serious, because I felt that she was very vulnerable at the time. I asked him not to take advantage of her. Simon smiled and asked me whether there was anything going on between Maggie and me, and I, of course, told him there wasn't. He then said that I shouldn't worry about Maggie, that she was a big girl and could handle herself, but told me that I shouldn't worry, that he would "be gentle." I must have visibly bristled, because he then said, "Don't worry, everything will work out fine." Simon then moved on to other matters involving the litigation section administration, signaling that the conversation about Maggie was over.

During the early spring of YR-3, it became obvious to me that a relationship other than professional was developing between Maggie and Simon. They were always out of town together on the NCW case, and they were inseparable when they were in the office. The rumors of another Simon Clark affair started to buzz around the office, and although I wasn't certain that anything was going on, the signs were all there.

At the same time the NCW case was apparently progressing very well, and according to Simon, Maggie had performed brilliantly. When the case settled on extremely favorable terms to NCW in June of YR-3, the client was so happy that the entire litigation team and spouses were invited to a week's vacation in the Bahamas at the client's expense. It was at this vacation that the affair between Simon and Maggie became public knowledge within the firm. According to others from the firm, Maggie and Simon were in each other's company constantly, from the earliest in the morning until the latest at night. They were also seen strolling arm in arm on the beach. When they returned, their relationship was obvious to everyone.

Given Simon's history, I felt that it was my responsibility as Maggie's friend and one of her mentors to counsel her about the risk attendant her relationship with Simon Clark. I asked Maggie whether she was aware of Simon's history with other women at the firm and she told me that she was. She told me that this time it was different, that Simon was going to leave his wife once his youngest son went away to college. I responded by saying something like "he's said that before," and Maggie told me she didn't want to discuss the matter any further. I did tell her that I hoped everything worked out for her, but that if it didn't that I didn't think that I could protect her interests at the firm. She looked sort of stunned, but just said thanks for my concern and I left. My statement to her was meant to convey the fact that there was some risk that her future at the firm would be compromised if it was viewed that her continued employment was contrary to Simon Clark's wishes. I can't say that Simon ever personally got an associate or paralegal with whom he was romantically involved dismissed from the firm, but I do believe that my partners would do whatever they thought was necessary to keep Simon Clark happy. After all, he was a major source of business for the firm, and we couldn't afford to lose him. I also know of no woman at the firm, either lawyer or paralegal, who survived professionally after an affair with Simon Clark.

Because of the work Maggie had done on NCW, as reported effusively by Simon Clark, and maybe because some of the lower level partners wanted to get on Simon's good side, Maggie was very much in demand for very high-quality assignments during the summer of YR-3. She apparently performed very well because all reports on her during her sixth-year evaluation process were glowing. In addition, the general counsel at NCW wrote a letter congratulating the entire litigation team, but giving special praise to Maggie. (SEE EXHIBIT 6) Several of the other partners in the litigation section even congratulated me on my good judgment in backing Maggie so strongly the previous year. Because of the high praise for her work and enormous number of billable hours, Maggie was graded at the A level for her sixth year, which as I said is a strong positive indicator for a favorable partnership decision in the seventh year. We, of course, informed Maggie of that fact and she seemed very pleased. Simon came around the desk and gave her a big hug and a kiss. Maggie looked a little embarrassed that Simon did that when I was in the room, so I just congratulated her and went back to my office.

During the fall of YR-3, Maggie was assigned to work on another case for NCW on which I was the lead partner. It was no where near as complex as the one the previous year, but it did give her another chance to show her talent. It also involved a similar issue of protecting NCW's trade secrets that was involved in the previous case that Maggie handled. She took good advantage of the opportunity and performed very well, at least during the fall of YR-3.

In the early part of YR-2, the inevitable happened and Simon Clark ended his affair with Maggie Polisi. Maggie went into an apparently rather deep depression. For the next several months her work was off and she seemed to be constantly suffering from a cold or the flu. As a result, the requests for her to work on cases also dropped-off. It's possible that the drop-off in work requests was also a result of the rather public breakup of Simon and Maggie. Just as some partners might try to curry favor with Simon by asking for Maggie when they knew she was involved with him, the opposite might also be true. I do not believe that Simon Clark was directly responsible for the drop-off in Maggie's assignments in that I never heard anyone say that Simon had approached them, but as I said, my partners might have reacted to what they thought was what Simon wanted. I just don't know.

At any rate, when I started to collect information for a partnership vote by the litigation section on the four people eligible for partnership that year, I started to receive some negative evaluations of Maggie's work. I also noted that her billable hours were sharply lower. She had billed 850 hours for September YR-3 through January YR-2 and only 550 hours for the four months leading up to her evaluation. In addition I started hearing questions again about her toughness and resiliency, and her ability to not let personal matters interfere with her work. There were even some questions raised about her intellectual ability, which I hadn't heard since Maggie's first year with the firm. And even though the NCW case should have answered any questions about how she performed when in unfamiliar settings, those criticisms also resurfaced, especially from Jayne Post.

I can't prove that Simon Clark did or said anything overtly about Maggie that caused the negative evaluations. He really wouldn't need to. After he and Maggie broke up, it was public information and some of my colleagues might have evaluated Maggie negatively to try to please Simon Clark. The breakup could certainly explain her drop-off in assignments as many of my partners wouldn't want to appear to weigh in favor of Maggie if there was a problem with Simon.

I approached Maggie with the bad news I was receiving. While I was not specific, I gave her the gist of the negative comments I was receiving about her. I also noted the sharp drop-off in billable hours. Maggie said that she just hadn't gotten a lot of assignments. I asked her why she hadn't come to me, and she said she really didn't think anything of it at the time, that she thought it was just a down work cycle. I wish she had said something or I had been more attentive. Lack of billables became a strong issue for Maggie's opponents. I gave her my best advice and told her that in my opinion it was not a good idea to push for partnership that year. I did tell her that if she chose to go forward that I would support her nomination for partnership by the litigation section, but that she would be in a much better position if she waited a year and repeated her sixth year performance. I assured her I would make certain she got the right assignments to showcase her talents. She didn't speak right away, and when she did, she asked whether Simon Clark had anything to do with her negative evaluation. When I didn't answer immediately she just said "never mind, I'll get back to you in a couple of days," and I left her office.

Several days later Maggie came by my office and told me that she wanted to go forward with a decision that year. I again tried to talk her out of it, but her mind was made up so I told her I'd do what she wished, and that she had my support. Simon had asked me to prepare the evaluation of Maggie and I did. Her evaluation was really in two parts. Her work was excellent during the fall, and then fell off in the winter and spring. As a result, I graded her at the B level.

The four people up for partnership nomination that year from the litigation section were Roger Kramer, Mark Hancock, Michael DeAngelo, and Maggie. The meeting began on a Thursday afternoon with a consideration of Michael DeAngelo. Mike had consistently been graded at the B level in his evaluations. Although not regarded as a superstar, he was considered as a rock-solid performer with uniformly good skills. There was some question about his ability to attract business and also about how he did on client relations. The question about client relations seemed to hang up the partnership and we went round and round on the matter. There was also the usual argument about whether being solid is enough, especially in a year when there were other candidates for partnership who had all scored in the A range, at least for one year. In the end, the partnership sent me back to Mike with a suggestion that he hold off for another year. The next year's class was not nearly so strong, and it would also give Mike another year to improve his evaluation. Although reluctant, Mike accepted the recommendation and withdrew for consideration in YR-2. As it turned out it was a very good move on his part as the reports on Mike's performance for the second half of YR-2 were terrific and continued through YR-1. In addition he was able to attract a good sized client to the firm. I understand that he eventually was made a partnership offer in June of YR-1.

Mark Hancock was an easy case. He too consistently received solid B evaluations, and although not brilliant was a solid performer. What distinguished Mark was his courtroom ability. During the spring of YR-2, he conducted devastating cross-examinations of several witnesses that his mentor credited for winning the case in a very important interference with contract matter for one of our best clients. The client was present during the examinations, and specifically requested that Mark be on any trial team for a case for that client. His trial performance rated him an A for his seventh year, and the client's insistence on his being on future trial teams made him a lock for partnership. He was nominated after a brief discussion, that mostly praised his abilities.

Roger Kramer was next and he, too, was an easy case. Roger was generally considered one of the smartest lawyers in the firm. He had received A evaluations in both his fifth and sixth years. Roger was also very personable and did very well with the clients on whose cases he worked. He was also the son of the president of one of our better clients, who we felt we would certainly lose if Roger was not with the firm. His billable hours were good, but if he had a weakness it was in that area. The only real question with Roger was whether he should have received a partnership offer in his sixth year. As expected, Roger breezed through.

The meeting then adjourned until Friday afternoon for the consideration of Maggie's candidacy. The meeting began at approximately 3 P.M. and lasted until 8 P.M.. Maggie had a number of very strong supporters, including myself, who thought she possessed a great combination of skills and that she would do great work on anything to which she was assigned. Her detractors raised all of the issues I mentioned before, Jayne Post being one of the most vociferous, and the debate was long and rancorous. Simon Clark, who chaired the meeting as chair of the section spoke very little. He did speak about Maggie's work on the NCW case in glowing terms, but admitted that Maggie's performance in YR-2 was troublesome. As chair of the section, he was not required to vote, but announced that he was going to abstain in the vote. His abstention, in my opinion, was the equivalent of a negative vote and probably was one of the determining factors in the outcome. In the end, however, the feeling that Maggie had been inconsistent in her performance, that in the view of some, reflected a lack of toughness and resiliency, plus the fact that she was not in a position to attract any business to the firm, carried the day. In a close vote her nomination for partnership was denied. I tried to get the partnership to allow her another year to improve her performance, but the litigation partners seemed to not have the stomach for a repeat of that meeting in a year. I was told to inform Maggie that she had six months to find another position.

I found Maggie in her office when the meeting ended. She took the news fairly hard. She asked if she could have another year to improve, but I told her that the decision was final. She did ask about what Simon's position at the meeting was, and I told her that I couldn't divulge individual comments as a matter of policy. I told her I was sorry, that I had done my best, but that there was nothing I could do.

After the meeting, I ran into Simon Clark outside his office. He asked me to come in for a drink which I did. He asked if I had gotten up with Maggie and I told him I had, and that she had taken the news pretty hard. He knew that Maggie was a favorite of mine and he asked how I was doing. Something snapped, and I lit into him. I told him that he was an egomaniac and that if he had exercised a little control of his libido that Maggie would be a partner today. I told him that he was a real jerk and that he had ruined a terrific legal career. Simon looked shocked. I had never talked to him that way before. He didn't deny my accusation, but he did say that it was Maggie who had ended the relationship, not him, and that he was sorry about how it had worked out. He said that he knew how I felt about Maggie and again said he was sorry, but this time to me. I told Simon that I would draft a recommendation letter for him concerning Maggie, in order to help her in securing a new position. He said that was fine. I then got up and walked out of Simon's office.

Ever since that day my relationship with Simon Clark has been different. Although we still interacted on business matters in a fairly regular way, the closeness we once had was gone, and, to be honest, I lost some respect for him. I think the same is true at the firm, because in September of YR-2, Simon was replaced as the chief of the litigation section after only three years in the position. The normal term for that position is five years. When the announcement was made by the Executive Committee of the firm of the change in leadership, it was couched in an explanation that Simon's trial schedule was too demanding to allow him sufficient time to administer the section, but the gossip in the firm is that the whole situation with Maggie was the straw that broke the camel's back as far as tolerance for Simon's dalliances. The new chief of the division is Rob Bryant. He asked me to stay on as deputy for purposes of continuity and I agreed to do so.

Maggie did not handle the situation of her firing well. Although she interviewed for jobs with other firms, nothing came of it. Originally I thought that her confidence had been undermined by the whole episode at P & G, and that probably affected her interviewing skills. I now know that in a couple of circumstances that Simon Clark had done her in with a poor reference letter. I only found out about the letters in January of YR-1 when Maggie called me to, tell me that she had a copy of a letter written by Simon to John Randall of the Morrison firm in Nita City which was far from complimentary. She read the letter to me, including some hand written comments that I now recognize to be in Simon's handwriting. (SEE EXHIBIT 11) I felt really bad about this because I had given Maggie a copy of the letter that I had drafted for Simon's signature, and had encouraged her to use him as a reference. (SEE EXHIBIT 10) I know that he had never been vindictive in any previous ending of an affair, so I was really surprised that he was regarding Maggie. When I confronted him with the fact that he didn't use my letter, Simon became very defensive and told me to mind my own business. Since that time I have lost what respect I had for Simon personally, although I have to concede to him his legal abilities.

I also know that Maggie tried to get a teaching job. Although she had some interviews at the law school hiring convention, the only thing that came of it initially was an adjunct teaching position at the University of Nita School of Law. Because I knew that adjuncts did not make much money, I offered to help Maggie out financially with whatever kind of loan she needed. She turned down my offer. Eventually Maggie ended up with teaching offers from both Nita University and Conwell University, although it took a while for them to come in. I'm happy to say that she returned to her and my alma mater, where I'm sure she will be a great success.

I also know that she filed a complaint against the firm with the EEOC. Although we did not talk directly about that fact at the time, the firm did receive notice of her allegations in the summer of YR-2. (SEE EXHIBIT 14) As the deputy of the litigation section, I was contacted to be sure to maintain whatever files we still had on Maggie and the other people who came up for partner in YR-2. We had the paragraph evaluations on Maggie and Mike DeAngelo because they were still associates at the time the firm received the EEOC letter. Because Mark Hancock and Roger Kramer had been made partners by that time, the only records we had on them for their years as associates were on their grades and their billable hours. The same was true of former associates from Maggie's class who had left the firm. (SEE EXHIBITS 7A and 7B) The firm returned the EEOC notice with a general denial written by Rob Bryant. (SEE EXHIBIT 15) Sometime in early January of YR-1 we received a copy of the EEOC's "right to sue" letter that was sent to Maggie. (SEE EXHIBIT 16)

Maggie resigned in December of YR-2 when her six-month grace period with the firm ended. I asked if there was anything I could do and she told me no, that she thought everything would work out. As I said, I know I told her that if she needed a loan I was always available. She thanked me but said that she didn't think that would be necessary. I told her that I was aware of her complaint to the EEOC and said that I would be willing to testify on her behalf if the need ever arose. She gave me a hug and left the firm.

The whole matter with Maggie Polisi has left a sour taste in my mouth for the politics of P & G, so when I was approached by NCW about my current job, I pursued the opportunity. I was surprised that it was so easy for me to leave P & G, but I guess the time was right. I have a terrific job at NCW where I oversee the entire legal department of about twenty-five lawyers, and also oversee our litigation which is farmed out to P & G. Simon Clark still handles our most important matters and I interact with him professionally, but we have no personal relationship any longer. I have not talked to him about Maggie's lawsuit against the firm, nor have I talked with P & G's lawyers.

When I got the job at NCW, one of the first people I tried to hire into our legal department was Maggie Polisi. At the time I offered her the job, in May of YR-1, she had already accepted the teaching position at Nita University, so she turned me down. I told her that there would always be a position for her at NCW if she ever changed her mind. Maggie and I continue to see each other socially from time to time. We are good friends. I'll have to admit, because you've asked, that I would be interested in a romantic relationship with her, but we have never interacted in that way, and I don't expect that we ever will.

STATEMENT OF RACHEL LEVIN

My name is Rachel Levin. I am forty-five years old and live at 212 West Woolsey Way in Nita City with my husband David. Our children Greg and Melissa, who are twins, are first-year law students at Nita University School of Law here in Nita City. David is a lawyer who is a civil side Assistant United States Attorney. I work in the law firm of Cooperman & Jones as an office manager for the litigation portion of the practice. I have been working at Cooperman & Jones since YR-4. I have a bachelors degree in business administration from Nita State University, which I received in YR-23. I began work at the Nita Stock Exchange that year, but left in YR-22 when my twins were born. I stayed out of the job market until YR-15, when the twins were in the second grade.

At that time, I accepted a job offer from an old friend of the family, Charles Milton, to come work for him at the law firm of Parker & Gould. Charles persuaded me to join the work force to work for him as his administrative assistant. Although I had no experience working in a law firm, I had been around lawyers all my life. My mom was a graduate of Nita University School of Law and she practiced law in the U. S. Attorney's Office for many years until she retired in YR-3. She introduced me to my husband, who was a clerk for one of the federal judges at the time we met. My dad was also in the U. S. Attorney's Office for a while until he was elected as a Superior Court judge in Nita City. He also retired in YR-3, and my parents now live in West Palm Beach, Florida.

My job for Mr. Milton was as an administrative assistant. He was a litigator at the firm, so my responsibilities included supervising his secretarial work, maintaining his calendar as to scheduling all of his depositions, court appearances, travel arrangements, etc. I also handled communication between Mr. Milton and other lawyers, both partners and associates, as well as paralegals who worked on his cases. Mr. Milton was a contemporary of my parents, having gone to law school with them, and was in his mid- to late-fifties when I wen to work for him. He was a senior litigator at P & G and was involved in numerous cases, but probably spent most of his time in attracting and keeping clients for the firm. As a result, I also was responsible for maintaining his active business/social schedule.

Earlier this year, my son was home for dinner on Sunday and mentioned that he thought his Civil Procedures professor was a terrific teacher. He also said that according to her bio she had worked at Parker & Gould during the time I was there. He said the professor's name was Professor Polisi. I asked what her first name was and he said it was Margaret but that he heard one of her colleagues refer to her as Maggie. As it turned out, I recalled Maggie Polisi from my time at P & G.

When Ms. Polisi was an associate, Charles Milton was the chair of the litigation section of the firm. As part of his job he was responsible for accumulating information and then evaluating each litigation associate on a yearly basis. I recall Ms. Polisi from that process, mainly because during one of her evaluations, she challenged one of the evaluations she received from one of the people she worked for, and there were several meetings between Polisi and Charles about the evaluation. I don't remember which evaluation it was, but it would have been in the time that Charles was the Chair of the Litigation Section. I also recall that after that, Charles used Ms. Polisi's services on several cases and that she had done quite well for him, but that is just a vague memory and I can't recall any of the specifics.

I told all of this to Greg, and he told me that the word at the law school was the Professor Polisi was fired by P & G because she wouldn't have sex with one of the partners, and that she had sued the firm. He asked me what kind of place I worked for because he was sure that Professor Polisi was in the right. I told Greg that as far as I knew the only partner that was capable of such activity was Simon Clark.

Clark had a reputation as a real sexual predator in the firm and his antics were well known. Even though he was a married man with several children, a week didn't go by that there wasn't a rumor about him going after some young woman at the firm. The rumors had some basis to them; of that I'm sure.

I know for a fact that about ten years ago Clark forced a fine young woman out of the firm. Her name was Carol Merritt. Carol was a young associate at the time. She was married to a nice young man. I met her at the office when she came to meet with Charles about work she was doing for him on his cases. I met her husband at a party celebrating a big win in one of Charles' case on which she was a member of the litigation team. He seemed like a very nice young man. I remember having a conversation of some duration with Carol and her husband at the party. Unlike some associates who wouldn't waste their time with someone other than a partner at such a gathering, Carol and her husband were most cordial to me and my husband, and talked with both of us about a number of things, including my husband David's and my Mom's experiences at the U. S. Attorney's Office.

After that time, Carol would always make a point of stopping by to say hello when her work brought her to Charles' office or the nearby office of another partner. She did some other work for Charles, but I can't recall anything specific about how she did on those cases. I know about Carol's affair with Clark. It was common knowledge in the firm.

Clark apparently swept Carol off her feet, and persuaded her to leave her husband and move into an apartment that I'm sure Clark paid for. It was obvious that Carol was uncomfortable with the situation, but I guess she didn't know how to turn Clark down.

At some point, I don't know exactly when or how, Clark dumped Carol and she fell really hard. Fortunately, her husband took her back. It was obvious that he truly loved her. But Carol never returned to the firm. It was common knowledge that Clark didn't like to have his former conquests around the firm. I don't have any specific information of this, but that was the word around the firm. I can't remember any of their names, but several times I heard that women associates or paralegals who Clark preyed on, were forced out of the firm after he no longer had any use for them.

I never saw or heard from Carol after that. I know that Charles wrote several letters on her behalf to firms in Washington, D.C where she and her husband moved. I remember Charles saying that he felt somewhat responsible for what happened to Carol, because Charles had recommended Carol to Clark for a case somewhere out of town. It was during that case that Clark made his move on Carol. For a smart lawyer, Carol was young and not very worldly (she had married her high school sweetheart after graduating from college), so she never really had a chance with the likes of Clark.

I know that Clark's antics were well known in the firm. As Charles Milton's administrative assistant, I was asked by Charles to take notes for him during meetings of the firm's Executive Committee of which he was a member. Those notes were for his personal use and I don't have any idea if they still exist. Charles was a stickler for throwing out paper after it was of no further use, so my guess is those notes were destroyed years ago.

I specifically recall that when Charles was finishing his term as Chair of the Litigation Section of the firm (he served from YR-10 until YR-5), that the topic of Clark as Charles' successor was the topic of conversation, both around the firm and specifically in the firm's Executive Committee meeting. Clark apparently wanted the position of the Chair of the section, and the Committee felt hard pressed not to give it to him.

Despite his obvious failings and lack of morality, Clark was generally regarded as the top litigator and trial lawyer in the firm. I know that Charles often took Clark along when dealing with current clients and trying to attract new clients to the firm. Charles often referred to Clark as the next great "rainmaker" (one who attracts business to the firm) for P & G. At the meetings leading up to Clark's selection as Chair, this was discussed openly in both the Executive

Committee and in the firm's rumor mill. The Executive Committee also discussed, as did others informally, that the only drawbacks to Clark as the Chair was that it might take away from his practice time, and whether it was wise to make Clark the Chair, who would have the responsibility of evaluating all the young associates in the firm, including the women. I remember Charles saying in the Executive Committee that having Clark evaluating women associates was like "having the fox guard the henhouse."

In the end, the Committee gave Clark his wish and he was named the Chair of the Litigation Section. Cliff Fuller, a very talented young partner with a good head on his shoulders who was Clark's protege, was appointed as Clark's Deputy Chair. The hope in the Committee was that Fuller could both lessen Clark's administrative load thereby keeping him available for practice and client cultivation, and assist in keeping Clark from going after the young women associates.

After my conversation with Greg, I checked with a couple of my friends at P & G to see if Professor Polisi was suing the firm, and they confirmed she was. I was told that she was suing both Clark and the firm for not being made partner, and that she claimed that Clark had harassed her and that the firm knew about it and did nothing to stop him. That was consistent, of course, with what I knew of Clark and the way the rest of the firm treated him like he could do no wrong.

I did not know of the lawsuit until I talked to Greg and checked it out with my old friends at P & G. As I said, I work at Cooperman & Jones now. I left P & G in YR-4 when Charles Milton died right after his 68th birthday. Charles' death was shocking to me and my family, and was the main reason that my parents decided to retire shortly thereafter. The firm informed me shortly after Charles' death that they would try to place me within the firm or help me get a job outside the firm. I opted for the latter, and got my position at Cooperman & Jones after being recommended to them by Cliff Fuller at P & G. I have no feelings, positive or negative, towards the firm now that Charles is no longer there.

As it turns out, I found out that Cliff Fuller, who had helped me get my current job, had also left the firm and had taken an executive position at Nita Computer World, one of P & G's best clients. The word from my friends at P & G was that Cliff left over the treatment of the firm of Professor Polisi. Shortly after finding this out, I contacted Cliff, and he confirmed what I had heard about Professor Polisi's lawsuit and said that he had agreed to act as a witness for Ms. Polisi. I told Cliff what I have just told you and he put me in touch with you. I have voluntarily given this statement to you, and I am available to testify at a deposition or trial, if necessary.

EXHIBITS

TABLE OF EXHIBITS

EXHIBIT 1

RESUME
MARGARET M. POLISI

EDUCATION:

University of Nita, B.A. Political Science, YR-19
Honors: Phi Beta Kappa

University of Nita School of Law, J.D., YR-9
Honors: Magna Cum Laude; Mary & William Walsh Award
For Legal Scholarship (Graduated First in Class); Thomas Knox
Award for Excellence in Law Review Editing.
Activities: Nita University Law Review, YR-12 – YR-9, Articles
Editor, Volume 82.

EMPLOYMENT:

University of Nita School of Law, Nita City
Associate Professor of Law, Since YR-1

Parker & Gould, Four Independence Square, Nita City
Associate – YR-9 – YR-2 – Worked on the full range civil litigation
matters. Duties included research, pretrial and trial writing, taking and
defending depositions, arguing motions, and examination of witnesses.
Litigation Law Clerk – YR-12 – YR-9
Litigation Paralegal – YR-17 – YR-12

PUBLICATIONS:

WORK PRODUCT AND THE RIGHT TO REFRESHING DOCU-
MENTS: SOMETHING'S GOT TO GIVE, 89 U. Nita L. Rev 45, (YR-
2).

LAWYER CONFLICTS OF INTEREST IN MULTI-PARTY ANTI-
TRUST LITIGATION, 58 Conwell U. L. Rev, YR-1.

COURSES TAUGHT:

Civil Procedure, Evidence, Seminar on Complex Civil Litigation

PERSONAL:

Address: 7010 Greenhill Road
Nita City, Nita

Phone: 555-8949 (Work)
555-2892 (Home)
Two Children: David and Maureen
Excellent Health. Enjoy tennis, hiking, water sports, and travel.

EXHIBIT 2

—— PARKER & GOULD ——
Four Independence Square
Nita City, Nita

July 1, YR-9

Ms. Margaret Polisi
Parker & Gould
Four Independence Square
Nita City, Nita

Dear Ms. Polisi,

This is to confirm that you have accepted a position with the law firm of Parker & Gould as an associate in our litigation department. Your beginning annual salary will be $85,000.00.

You will be required to assume the normal responsibilities of an associate with the firm, and it is understood that your position with the firm will be evaluated each year.

As you are currently employed as a law clerk, you are familiar with the benefits package at P & G, so I will not cover them specifically in this letter. If you have any questions concerning our benefits package, please contact Mary Williamson in our benefits office. As you know, you will receive one month's salary to compensate you for your time spent in studying for the bar examination.

Please notify me at your earliest convenience as to your anticipated starting date with the firm. We look forward to your coming on board.

If the above terms and conditions are acceptable to you, please indicate same by signing and returning one copy of this letter.

Welcome.

Sincerely,

Charles Milton, Chair
Litigation Section

Signed: *Margaret Polisi*
Margaret Polisi

Date: 7-10-YR-9

—— *PARKER & GOULD* ——
Four Independence Square
Nita City, Nita

MEMORANDUM

TO: M. Polisi File

FROM: C. Milton, Chair Litigation Section   *CM*

RE: First-Year Evaluation

DATE: September 10, YR-8

****

GRADE: C

HOURS: 1770

NARRATIVE: Ms. Polisi had an acceptable first year. Writing
           needs improvement. Hours are acceptable for a first-
           year associate but we expect improvement here also.
           Bright, articulate. Two associates in class with a B,
           seven others with a C. 3 percent raise.

—— PARKER & GOULD ——
Four Independence Square
Nita City, Nita

MEMORANDUM

TO: M. Polisi File

FROM: C. Milton, Chair Litigation Section   *CM*

RE: Second-Year Evaluation

DATE: September 13, YR-7

****

GRADE: B

HOURS: 1960

NARRATIVE: Ms. Polisi had a good second year. Improvement noted
           in both writing style and in billable hours. Remains
           some small question concerning analytical ability.
           Some questions raised concerning aggressiveness.
           Three other associates in class with a B. 5 percent
           raise.

—— *PARKER & GOULD* ——
Four Independence Square
Nita City, Nita

MEMORANDUM

TO: M. Polisi File

FROM: C. Milton, Chair Litigation Section   *CM*

RE: Third-Year Evaluation

DATE: September 11, YR-6

****

GRADE: B

HOURS: 2020

NARRATIVE: Ms. Polisi had a good third year. Research and writing
            skills are acceptable. Hours acceptable. Positive com-
            ments on analytical skill with one exception. Still some
            questions concerning aggressiveness. Three other associ-
            ates in class with a B. 5 percent raise.

—— PARKER & GOULD ——
Four Independence Square
Nita City, Nita

MEMORANDUM

TO: M. Polisi File

FROM: C. Milton, Chair Litigation Section *CM*

RE: Fourth-Year Evaluation

DATE: September 13, YR-5

****

GRADE: B

HOURS: 2040

NARRATIVE: Ms. Polisi had a good year at the firm. Research, analysis and writing skills remain strong. Still some question concerning toughness and lack of aggressiveness. Question raised concerning failure to travel outside of Nita area for extended periods. Hours acceptable. Four other associates in class with a B. 5 percent raise. $10,000.00 market adjustment.

—— *PARKER & GOULD* ——
Four Independence Square
Nita City, Nita

MEMORANDUM

TO: M. Polisi File

FROM: S. Clark, Chair Litigation Section *SC*

RE: Fifth-Year Evaluation

DATE: September 14, YR-4

****

GRADE: C

HOURS: 1830

NARRATIVE: Ms. Polisi had a mediocre year at the firm. Her billable hours are not acceptable. Also received some negative comments on quality of analytical ability. Given option of leaving firm with good recommendation, attempted placement with client or attempt to improve substantially. Chooses to remain with firm. One associate in class with an A. Two associates in class with a B. Six other associates in class with a C. 3 percent raise.

—— *PARKER & GOULD* ——
Four Independence Square
Nita City, Nita

MEMORANDUM

TO: M. Polisi File

FROM: S. Clark, Chair Litigation Section *SC*

RE: Sixth-Year Evaluation

DATE: September 14, YR-3

****

GRADE: A

HOURS: 2300

NARRATIVE: Ms. Polisi had an excellent year. Billable hours are
            very good. NCW complimentary on her work in recent
            case. Good candidate for partnership. One other
            associate in class with an A. 7 percent raise.

—— *PARKER & GOULD* ——
Four Independence Square
Nita City, Nita

MEMORANDUM

TO: M. Polisi

FROM: C. Fuller, Deputy Chair, Litigation Section *C. F.*

RE: Partnership Evaluation - Seventh Year

DATE: June 2, YR-2

****

GRADE: B

HOURS: 1445 (As of June 1, YR-2)

NARRATIVE: Ms. Polisi had a good fall, and a mediocre winter and
spring. Billable hours were fine (895) for September
YR-3. January YR-2 drop-off to 550 hours for February
YR-2 through May YR-2, which are not acceptable for
that period. Some questions raised concerning quality
of written product and toughness. Advised to put
partnership decision over until YR-1. Ms. Polisi
declines advice. Two associates in partnership class
with an A. One other associate in partnership class
with a B.

June 15, YR-2 - Partnership nomination by Litigation
Section declined. Given until December 15, YR-2, to
find another position.

——— *PARKER & GOULD* ———
Four Independence Square
Nita City, Nita

September 20, YR-8

Ms. Margaret Polisi
Parker & Gould
Four Independence Square
Nita City, Nita

Dear Ms. Polisi,

This is to confirm that your salary for the year September YR-8 through September YR-7 will be $87,550.00. This represents a merit raise of 3 percent.

Your contributions to the firm are appreciated.

Sincerely,

Charles Milton, Chair
Litigation Section

—— *PARKER & GOULD* ——
Four Independence Square
Nita City, Nita

September 22, YR-7

Ms. Margaret Polisi
Parker & Gould
Four Independence Square
Nita City, Nita

Dear Ms. Polisi,

This is to confirm that your salary for the year September YR-7
through September YR-6 will be $91,928.00. This represents a merit
raise of 5 percent.

Your contributions to the firm are appreciated.

Sincerely,

Charles Milton, Chair
Litigation Section

—— *PARKER & GOULD* ——
Four Independence Square
Nita City, Nita

September 18, YR-6

Ms. Margaret Polisi
Parker & Gould
Four Independence Square
Nita City, Nita

Dear Ms. Polisi,

This is to confirm that your salary for the year September YR-6 through September YR-5 will be $96,525.00. This represents a merit raise of 5 percent.

Your contributions to the firm are appreciated.

Sincerely,

Charles Milton, Chair
Litigation Section

—— *PARKER & GOULD* ——
Four Independence Square
Nita City, Nita

September 21, YR-5

Ms. Margaret Polisi
Parker & Gould
Four Independence Square
Nita City, Nita

Dear Ms. Polisi,

This is to confirm that your salary for the year September YR-5
through September YR-4 will be $111,352.00. This represents a
merit raise of 5 percent and a market adjustment of $10,000.00.

Your contributions to the firm are appreciated.

Sincerely,

Charles Milton, Chair
Litigation Section

—— *PARKER & GOULD* ——
Four Independence Square
Nita City, Nita

September 22, YR-4

Ms. Margaret Polisi
Parker & Gould
Four Independence Square
Nita City, Nita

Dear Ms. Polisi,

This is to confirm that your salary for the year September YR-4 through September YR-3 will be $114,693.00. This represents a merit raise of 3 percent.

The firm values your contributions and we look forward to a productive year.

Sincerely yours,

Simon Clark

Simon Clark, Chair
Litigation Section

—— PARKER & GOULD ——
Four Independence Square
Nita City, Nita

September 24, YR-3

Ms. Margaret Polisi
Parker & Gould
Four Independence Square
Nita City, Nita

Dear Ms. Polisi,

This is to confirm that your salary for the year September YR-3 through September YR-2 will be $122,721. This represents a merit raise of 7 percent.

The firms values your contributions and we look forward to a productive year.

Warm regards,

Simon Clark

Simon Clark, Chair
Litigation Section

—— PARKER & GOULD ——
Four Independence Square
Nita City, Nita

MEMORANDUM

TO: M. DeAngelo File

FROM: C. Milton, Chair Litigation Section   *CM*

RE: First-Year Evaluation

DATE: September 9, YR-8

****

GRADE: B

HOURS: 1880

NARRATIVE: Mr. DeAngelo had a good first year. Hours are good
           for a first year. Writing style needs work. Analyti-
           cal skills acceptable. Good aggressiveness in seeking
           out assignments. One other associate in class with a
           B. 5 percent raise.

—— *PARKER & GOULD* ——
Four Independence Square
Nita City, Nita

MEMORANDUM

TO: M. DeAngelo File

FROM: C. Milton, Chair Litigation Section   *CM*

RE: Second-Year Evaluation

DATE: September 11, YR-7

****

GRADE: B

HOURS: 1910

NARRATIVE: Mr. DeAngelo had a good second year. His billable hours are acceptable. Writing style improving. Analysis acceptable. Good aggressiveness and mental toughness. Three other associates in class with a B. 5 percent raise.

—— *PARKER & GOULD* ——
Four Independence Square
Nita City, Nita

MEMORANDUM

TO: M. DeAngelo File

FROM: C. Milton, Chair Litigation Section   *CM*

RE: Third-Year Evaluation

DATE: September 12, YR-6

****

GRADE: B

HOURS: 2100

NARRATIVE: Mr. DeAngelo had a good year. Hours at top of class.
            Writing style improved. Acceptable analytical abil-
            ity. Very tough and resilient. Three other associates
            in class with a B. 5 percent raise.

—— *PARKER & GOULD* ——
Four Independence Square
Nita City, Nita

MEMORANDUM

TO: M. DeAngelo File

FROM: C. Milton, Chair Litigation Section   *CM*

RE: Fourth-Year Evaluation

DATE: September 10, YR-5

****

GRADE: B

HOURS: 2220

NARRATIVE: Mr. DeAngelo had a good year. Billable hours at top of his class. Uniform good skills. Some question about how he will do in client relations. Good aggressiveness. Four other associates in class with a B. 5 percent raise. $10,000.00 market adjustment.

—— *PARKER & GOULD* ——
Four Independence Square
Nita City, Nita

MEMORANDUM

TO: M. DeAngelo File

FROM: S. Clark, Chair Litigation Section   *SC*

RE: Fifth-Year Evaluation

DATE: September 13, YR-4

****

GRADE: B

HOURS: 2260

NARRATIVE: Another solid year for Mr. DeAngelo. Hours at the top
              of class. Good candidate for partnership, but looking
              for spark. Some questions concerning client rela-
              tions. Skills uniformly good. One associate in class
              with an A. One other associate in class with a B. 5
              percent raise.

—— *PARKER & GOULD* ——
Four Independence Square
Nita City, Nita

MEMORANDUM

TO: M. DeAngelo File

FROM: S. Clark, Chair Litigation Section   *SC*

RE: Sixth-Year Evaluation

DATE: September 13, YR-3

****

GRADE: B

HOURS: 2210

NARRATIVE: Mr. DeAngelo has another solid year at the firm.
           Billable hours are among firm's highest for associ-
           ates. Skills uniformly good but not stellar in any
           particular area. Continuing question concerning
           client relations. Good partnership potential. Two
           associates in class with an A. One other associate in
           class with B. 5 percent raise.

—— *PARKER & GOULD* ——
Four Independence Square
Nita City, Nita

MEMORANDUM

TO: M. DeAngelo File

FROM: S. Clark, Chair Litigation Section   *SC*

RE: Partnership Evaluation - Seventh Year

DATE: June 2, YR-2

****

GRADE: B

HOURS: 1700 (As of June 1, YR-2)

NARRATIVE: Mr. DeAngelo is a solid performer. Has regained status as top billing associate. Solid in all respects. Only questions are concerning client relations and ability to attract and/or keep clients. Two associates in partnership class with an A. One other associate with a B.

June 15, YR-2 - On recommendation of litigation partnership, decision put over to June, YR-1. 5 percent raise effective June 1, YR-2.

—— *PARKER & GOULD* ——
Four Independence Square
Nita City, Nita

MEMORANDUM

TO: M. DeAngelo File

FROM: R. Bryant, Chair Litigation Section   *RB*

RE: Partnership Evaluation - Eighth Year

DATE: June 2, YR-1

****

GRADE: A

HOURS: 2380

NARRATIVE: Mr. DeAngelo had an excellent year. Skills are
           uniformly good. Billable hours are highest for all
           associates. Performed very well in complex trial in
           examination of experts. Attracted new client to the
           firm. One other associate in partnership class with
           an A.

           June 16, YR-1 - Partnership nomination made by
           litigation section.

EXHIBIT 6

NITA COMPUTER WORLD "A WORLD BETTER"
1550 SCIENCE DRIVE
NITA CITY, NITA

July 8, YR-3

Mr. Simon Clark
Parker & Gould
Four Independence Square
Nita City, Nita

Dear Simon:

I have just returned from a Board of Directors Meeting for the company and wanted to report how pleased the Board is over the outcome in our most recent litigation handled by you and your firm. As you may know, several of the companies who failed to settle the case were hit pretty hard by the jury in that case and the work of you and your team, together with your wise counsel saved us a great deal of money.

Please pass on my thanks to your litigation team. In particular, I should tell you that I was most impressed with the performance, as I observed it, of your associate, Maggie Polisi. She did a fine job in arguing for our trade secret protective order, the positive result of which positioned us well for settlement of the case. I do not know her status at the firm, but NCW would be pleased to have her work on other matters for us in the future. Specifically, we have been sued in a matter that is being handled by Cliff Fuller in which a similar issue of trade secrets is involved, and I hope that she can be assigned to that case.

I trust that you and your team enjoyed your recent trip. I'll get a full report when we meet next week.

Warm regards,

Howard Meltzer
Vice President
General Counsel

cc: Ms. Margaret Polisi
    Parker & Gould

—— *PARKER & GOULD* ——
Four Independence Square
Nita City, Nita

COMPILATION OF EMPLOYMENT RECORDS FOR ASSOCIATES ENTERING YR-9 WHILE ON PARTNERSHIP TRACK

ENTRIES SHOW NAME OF ASSOCIATE, GRADE & BILLABLE HOURS FOR EACH YEAR WITH FIRM

NAME	YR-8	YR-7	YR-6	YR-5	YR-4	YR-3	YR-2
DeAngelo, Michael	B 1880	B 1910	B 2100	B 2220	B 2260	B 2210	B 2250
Eisenberg, David	D 1740	D 1800					
Forsano, Elizabeth	C 1700	C 1820	C 1860	C 1900			
Hancock, Mark	C 1750	C 1850	B 2060	B 2160	B 2210	B 2190	A 1650*
Jenner, Jennifer	D 1650	C 1820					
Kramer, Roger	B 1850	B 1900	B 1910	B 1940	A 2070	A 2050	A 1590*
Levy, Esther	C 1790	C 1840	C 1890				
Lucas, Ralph	D 1740	C 1800	C 1810	C 1890	C 1940		
Marin, John	D 1710	D 1740					
Medovsky, Gregory	D 1740	C 1810	C 1860	C 1910	C 1960		

COMPILATION OF EMPLOYMENT RECORDS - ASSOCIATES ENTERING YR-9 (CONTINUE)

NAME	YR-8	YR-7	YR-6	YR-5	YR-4	YR-3	YR-2
Nathans, Howard	C 1760	C 1800	D 1780				
Opperheim, Richard	D 1650	C 1850	C 1950	P/A**			
Polisi, Margaret	C 1770	B 1960	B 2020	B 2040	C 1830	A 2300	B 1750
Polen, Craig	C 1780	C 1880					
Richards, Harriet	C 1780	C 1840	C 1880	C 1980			
Sherman, Gary	B 1850	B 1920	C 1880	B 2010			
Tomlinson, Mary	C 1800	C 1820	C 1890	P/A**			
Washburn, Peter	C 1740	C 1880	D 1650				
Wasilewski, Kathryn	C 1780	C 1860	C 1900	C 1930	C 1960		

* Elected to partnership, June, YR-2. Hours reflect those accumulated through June 1, YR-2.

**Accepted position as permanent associate with firm. No longer on partnership track.

EXHIBIT 8

—— *PARKER & GOULD* ——
Four Independence Square
Nita City, Nita

INCOMING PHONE LOG

NAME: S. Clark   **SECRETARY:** Cary Jones

DATE	PERSON CALLING	PHONE NUMBER	MESSAGE
7/9/-2	David Greenburg IRS	202-544-1770	Please call re: Tax Audit ✓
7/9/-2	Bill Grayson NCW	530-1000	Please call re: Cal. litigation ✓
7/9/-2	Mary Carson Nita Country Club	555-1444 member/guest	Please call re: tournament ✓
7/9/-2	John Randall Morrison & Farrow	555-5880 Polisi	Please call re: recommendation ✓
7/9/-2	Amanda	Home or car	Dinner with Mitchells ✓
7/9/-2	Gerry Mason Cooper & Davis	215-878-3000	Please call re: Rogers v. Preston Tools ✓

EXHIBIT 9

— PARKER & GOULD —
Four Independence Square
Nita City, Nita

INCOMING PHONE LOG

NAME: Simon Clark   **SECRETARY:** Cary Jones

DATE	PERSON CALLING	PHONE NUMBER	MESSAGE
7/15/-2	Bill Grayson NCW	530-1000	Call re: Cal. litigation ✓
7/15/-2	Harriet Miller Carter & Carroll	441-4100	Please call re: Polisi recommendation ✓
7/15/-2	Rob Bryant	x8110	Please call ✓
7/15/-2	Amanda	At Club	Dinner with Meltons ✓
7/15/-2	Roger Warren Melinson & Capps	487-6000	Please call re: Polisi recommendation ✓
7/15/-2	Andy Freeman Cooper & Davis	215-878-3000	Please call re: Rogers v. Preston Tools ✓ outstanding interrogatories

EXHIBIT 10

Simon –
This is the
recommendation
letter. C. F.

—— *PARKER & GOULD* ——
Four Independence Square
Nita City, Nita

Dear

It is with great pleasure that I write you concerning Ms. Margaret Polisi who has applied for a position with your firm. Over the past several years I have worked closely with her and feel well qualified to evaluate her abilities as a litigator.

Ms. Polisi came to us after a distinguished career at the University of Nita School of Law where she was an Editor of the Law Review and graduated first in her class. During her time at Parker & Gould she has worked on the most sophisticated of matters and has demonstrated enormous talent as a litigator.

She possesses analytical prowess, a talent for precision and persuasiveness in writing, and the ability to articulate her clients' positions in effective oral advocacy. She has, quite frankly, excelled in all areas of lawyering.

In addition to her superb skills, Ms. Polisi has shown excellent maturity and does very well in client interaction. In fact, in a recent case, involving one of our most sophisticated clients, she was commended by the client, in writing, at the successful conclusion of the case.

In closing, let me say that you will have a difficult time finding a better addition to your firm than Ms. Polisi. If I can be of further assistance, please do not hesitate to call.

Sincerely,

Simon Clark

EXHIBIT 11

—— *PARKER & GOULD* ——
Four Independence Square
Nita City, Nita

June 27, YR-2

Mr. John Randall
Morrison & Farrow
Four Courthouse Square
Nita City, Nita

No further interviews, not interested. JR

Dear John,

It is with great pleasure that I write in recommendation of Ms. Margaret Polisi for a position with your firm. Although my opportunities to work with her have been limited because of some travel restrictions she imposed, I have worked with her on several cases which provide me with an adequate basis to evaluate her abilities.

Ms. Polisi possesses a fine mind and generally applies it to her work. She has performed the full range of associate duties at the firm and her work has been well received by myself and my partners. Her analytical skills are solid, and she presents her analysis in a clear writing style. In addition, while her opportunities have been limited, she has taken and defended depositions and represented our clients in motion practice before various courts.

In closing, let me say that a decision to hire Ms. Polisi for an associate's position with your firm would be a good one. I am sure that you will be satisfied with her performance. If I can be of further assistance, please feel free to call.

Warm regards,

Simon Clark

Simon Clark, Chair
Litigation Section

P.S. John -- be careful on this one. Call me. SC

EXHIBIT 12

—— *PARKER & GOULD* ——
Four Independence Square
Nita City, Nita

July 7, YR-2

Ms. Harriet Miller
Carter & Carroll
410 Pine Street
Nita City, Nita

Dear Ms. Miller,

It is with great pleasure that I write in recommendation of Ms. Margaret Polisi for a position with your firm. Although my opportunities to work with her have been limited because of some travel restrictions she imposed, I have worked with her on several cases which provide me with an adequate basis to evaluate her abilities.

Ms. Polisi possesses a fine mind and generally applies it to her work. She has performed the full range of associate duties at the firm and her work has been well received by myself and my partners. Her analytical skills are solid, and she presents her analysis in a clear writing style. In addition, while her opportunities have been limited, she has taken and defended depositions and represented our clients in motion practice before various courts.

In closing, let me say that a decision to hire Ms. Polisi for an associate's position with your firm would be a good one. I am sure that you will be satisfied with her performance. If I can be of further assistance, please feel free to call.

Sincerely yours,

Simon Clark

Simon Clark, Chair
Litigation Section

EXHIBIT 13

—— *PARKER & GOULD* ——
Four Independence Square
Nita City, Nita

July 8, YR-2

Mr. Roger Warren
Melinson & Capps
1420 JFK Boulevard
Nita City, Nita

Dear Roger,

It is with great pleasure that I write in recommendation of Ms. Margaret Polisi for a position with your firm. Although my opportunities to work with her have been limited because of some travel restrictions she imposed, I have worked with her on several cases which provide me with an adequate basis to evaluate her abilities.

Ms. Polisi possesses a fine mind and generally applied it to her work. She has performed the full range of associate duties at the firm and her work has been well received by myself and my partners. Her analytical skills are solid, and she presents her analysis in a clear writing style. In addition, while her opportunities have been limited, she has taken and defended depositions and represented our clients in motion practice in various courts.

In closing, let me say that a decision to hire Ms. Polisi for an associate's position with your firm would be a good one. I am sure that you will be satisfied with her performance. If I can be of further assistance, please feel free to call.

Warm regards,

Simon Clark

Simon Clark, Chair
Litigation Section

*Spoke to S.C
- Not a good
lateral candidate.
R.W.*

EXHIBIT 14

EQUAL EMPLOYMENT OPPORTUNITY COMMISSION	PERSON FILING CHARGE Margaret Polisi

THIS PERSON (check one)

- [X] CLAIMS TO BE AGGRIEVED
- [ ] IS FILING ON BEHALF OF ANOTHER

DATE OF ALLEGED VIOLATION
Earliest

1/1/YR-2

Parker & Gould
Four Independence Square
Nita City, Nita

PLACE OF ALLEGED VIOLATION
Nita City, Nita

CHARGE NUMBER
YR-2-49985

NOTICE OF CHARGE OF DISCRIMINATION
(See EEOC "Rules and Regulations" before completing this Form)

You are hereby notified that a charge of employment discrimination has been filed against your organization under:

- [X] TITLE VII OF THE CIVIL RIGHTS ACT OF 1964

- [ ] THE AGE DISCRIMINATION IN EMPLOYMENT ACT OF 1967

- [ ] THE AMERICANS WITH DISABILITIES ACT

- [ ] THE EQUAL PAY ACT (29 U.S.C. SECT. 206(d)) investigation will be conducted concurrently with our investigation of this charge.

The boxes checked below apply to your organization:

1. [ ] No action is required on your part at this time.

2. [X] Please submit by <u>8/1/YR-2</u> a statement of your position with respect to the allegation(s) contained in this charge, with copies of any supporting documentation. This material will be made a part of the file and will be considered at the time that we investigate this charge. Your prompt response to this request will make it easier to conduct and conclude our investigation of this charge.

3. [ ] Please respond fully by _____ to the attached request for information which pertains to the allegations contained in this charge. Such information will be made a part of the file and will be considered by the Commission during the course of its investigation of the charge.

For further inquiry on this matter, please use the charge number shown above. Your position statement, your response to our request for information, or any inquiry you may have should be directed to:

Terry Mattoon
(Commission Representative)

555-4444
(Telephone Number)

[ ] Enclosure: Copy of Charge

BASIS OF DISCRIMINATION

[ ] RACE [ ] COLOR [X] SEX [ ] RELIGION [ ] NAT. ORIGIN [ ] AGE [ ] DISABILITY [ ] RETALIATION [ ] OTHER

CIRCUMSTANCES OF ALLEGED VIOLATION

Claimant states that she was denied partnership at the law firm of Parker & Gould because of her refusal to continue a sexual relationship with Simon Clark, a partner in the law firm of Parker & Gould. She further states that the law firm participated in the denial of partnership on that basis.

DATE	TYPED NAME/TITLE OF AUTHORIZED EEOC OFFICIAL	SIGNATURE
6/30/YR-2	Terry Mattoon	*Terry Mattoon*

EEOC FORM 131 (Rev. 08/92)

CHARGING PARTY'S COPY

EXHIBIT 15

—— *PARKER & GOULD* ——
Four Independence Square
Nita City, Nita

September 1, YR-2

Ms. Terry Mattoon
Equal Employment
Opportunity Commission
22 Constitution Plaza
Nita City, Nita

Dear Ms. Mattoon:

I am writing on behalf of the law firm of Parker & Gould in response to your correspondence of June 30, YR-2, in which you provided to us a Notice of Charge of Discrimination by Ms. Margaret Polisi.

Parker & Gould categorically denies that the negative partnership decision by the firm concerning Ms. Polisi was on any basis other than the merits. Ms. Polisi was denied partnership in the firm because her billable hours were not acceptable, the quality of her work was not acceptable, her ability to attract business to the firm was not acceptable, and because in times of personal crisis she was unable to adequately perform her job functions at the firm.

If you have any further questions concerning this unfounded allegation please feel free to contact me.

Sincerely,

Robert Bryant

Robert Bryant, Chair
Litigation Section

EXHIBIT 16

EQUAL EMPLOYMENT OPPORTUNITY COMMISSION
NOTICE OF RIGHT TO SUE
(Issued on request)

To: Ms. Margaret Polisi 7010 Greenhill Road Nita City, Nita	From: Equal Employment Opportunity Commission 22 Constitution Plaza Nita City, Nita
☐ On behalf of a person agrieved whose identity is *confidential* (29 C.F.R. 1601.7(a))	

Charge Number	EEOC Representative	Telephone number
YR-2-49985	Terry Mattoon	555-4444

(See the additional information attached to this form)

TO THE PERSON AGGRIEVED: This is your NOTICE OF RIGHT TO SUE. It is issued at your request. If you intend to sue the respondent(s) named in your charge, YOU MUST DO SO WITHIN NINETY (90) DAYS OF YOUR RECEIPT OF THIS NOTICE: OTHERWISE YOUR RIGHT TO SUE IS LOST.

☒ More than 180 days have expired since the filing of this charge.

☐ Less than 180 days have expired since the filing of this charge, but I have determined that the Commission will be unable to complete its process within 180 days from the filing of the charge.

☒ With the issuance of this NOTICE OF RIGHT TO SUE, the Commission is terminating its process with respect to this charge.

☐ It has been determined that the Commission will continue to investigate your charge.

☐ ADEA: While Title VII and the ADA require EEOC to issue this notice of right to sue before you can bring a lawsuit you may sue under the Age Discrimination in Employment ct (ADEA) any time 60 days after your charge was filed until **90 days after you received notice that EEOC has completed action on your charge.**

    ☐ **Because EEOC is closing your case,** your lawsuit under the ADEA must be brought within 90 days of your receipt of this notice. Otherwise, your right to sue is lost.

    ☐ **EEOC is continuing its investigation.** You will be notified when we have completed action and, if our notice will include notice of right to sue under the ADEA.

☐ EPA: While Title VII and the ADA require EEOC to issue this Notice of Right To Sue before you can bring a lawsuit you already have the right to sue under the Equal Pay Act (EPA) (You are not required to complain to any enforcement agency before bringing an EPA suit in court). EPA suits must be brought within 2 years (3 years for willful violations) of the alleged EPA underpayment.

I certify that this notice was mailed on the date set out below.

On Behalf of the Commission

_____12/28/YR-2_____
(Date Mailed)

_____Terry Mattoon_____
Terry Mattoon

Enclosures
  Information Sheet
  Copy of Charge

cc: Respondents

EEOC Form 161-B (Test 10/94)

EXHIBIT 17

—— *PARKER & GOULD* ——
Four Independence Square
Nita City, Nita

October 15, YR-2

Dean Martin Purcell
University of Nita
School of Law
One Campus Center
Nita City, Nita

Dear Marty,

It is with great pleasure that I write you concerning Ms. Margaret Polisi, who has applied for a teaching position at the law school. Over the past several years I have worked closely with her and feel well qualified to evaluate her abilities as a litigator, which I believe should translate over into the classroom.

Ms. Polisi came to us after a distinguished career at your school, where, as I am sure you know, she was an Editor of the Law Review and graduated first in her class. During her time at Parker & Gould she has worked on the most sophisticated of matters and has demonstrated enormous talent.

She possesses analytical prowess, a talent for precision and persuasiveness in writing, and the ability to articulate her clients' positions in effective oral advocacy. She has, quite frankly, excelled in all areas of lawyering.

In addition to her superb skills, Ms. Polisi has shown excellent maturity and does very well in client interaction. In fact, in a fairly recent case, involving one of our most sophisticated clients, she was commended by the client, in writing, at the successful conclusion of the case.

In closing, let me say that you will have a difficult time finding a better addition to your faculty than Ms. Polisi. If I can be of any further assistance, please to do not hesitate to call.

Please give my warmest regards to Ellen and the children.

Warm regards,

Simon Clark

Simon Clark

EXHIBIT 18

AFFIDAVIT OF JOHN RANDALL

My name is John Randall, and until recently I was a partner in the firm of Morrison & Farrow in Nita City. I have retired from the practice of law as of November 1, YR-1 and will be moving to France to live in the near future. I do not intend to return to the United States any time in the near future.

I have agreed to give this affidavit before this court reporter and counsel for both the plaintiff and defendants in the case of *Polisi v. Clark and Parker & Gould* in order to tell what I know about the facts of this case.

In the summer of YR-2 I received an impressive resume from an associate at Parker & Gould by the name of Margaret Polisi. I no longer have that resume but the document shown to me marked as Exhibit 1 looks familiar, although obviously, there were no job entries beyond her position at Parker & Gould. The resume also listed Simon Clark at P & G as a reference.

I have known Simon for over twenty years and I respect his opinion on legal talent, so I asked Ms. Polisi to have Simon send me a letter of recommendation. Shortly thereafter I received his letter of recommendation. Although the letter was not negative, I wouldn't call it a positive letter either. His evaluation of Ms. Polisi was apparently lukewarm. In addition, he included a handwritten note that I should take care regarding this candidate or something to that effect. Looking at what's been marked as Exhibit 11, that is the letter I received. The second handwritten note on the letter is in my handwriting.

When I received Simon's letter, I gave him a call and asked for an oral evaluation. He told me that Ms. Polisi had been turned down for partnership, a fact that I had assumed given her years at the firm, and the fact that she was applying for a job with us. He also told me that Ms. Polisi was not a good candidate for my practice, which was a white-collar-criminal practice, because there was reason to question her toughness and ability to cope with the stress inherent in my kind of practice. I then asked him whether she would be suitable for the civil litigation section of our firm where an opening had just occurred. He told me that in his opinion Ms. Polisi was not cut out for litigation of any sort, that she was just not reliable.

As a result of the letter and the phone call, I did not pursue hiring Ms. Polisi, nor did I refer her resume to the civil side of Morrison and Farrow.

Given her resume, absent the information from Simon Clark, we certainly would have interviewed Ms. Polisi for a position with our firm, on either the civil or criminal side. She seemed well qualified, at least on paper. Whether we would have hired her is an open question, and would have depended on her performance in the interview and whether we thought she would fit into the firm. Unlike P & G, we were then and are now a medium-sized law firm, so personality conflicts are a greater problem for us, and so the interview and our evaluation of how

EXHIBIT 18

Ms. Polisi would fit in with the other men and women at the firm would have been an important consideration.

Further the affiant sayeth not.

John Randall

Subscribed and sworn before me this 9th day of October, YR-1.

Mary Williams
Notary Public

SUPPLEMENTAL MATERIALS

SUPPLEMENTAL MATERIALS

SUMMARY OF CONTENTS

.

FIVE WAYS TO USE A DEPOSITION AT TRIAL

1. To Refresh Recollection

2. As Prior Testimony

3. For an Offer of Proof

4. As a Source of Admissions

5. For Impeachment by Prior Inconsistent Statement

WITNESS PREPARATION

LEGAL ETHICS

MODEL RULES OF PROFESSIONAL CONDUCT

PROBLEMS IN DEALING WITH OPPOSING COUNSEL AT DEPOSITION

ARTHUR J. HALL, PLAINTIFF, V. CLIFTON PRECISION, A DIVISION OF LITTON SYSTEMS, INC. CIV. A. NO. 92–5947

FIVE WAYS TO USE A DEPOSITION AT TRIAL

By ANTHONY J. BOCCHINO
and DAVID M. MALONE

I.

USE OF DEPOSITION TO REFRESH RECOLLECTION
Federal Rule of Evidence 612

Direct Examination of Margaret Polisi by the Plaintiff:

Q: Did your work on the NCW case require you to travel outside of Nita City during YR-4 and YR-3?

A: Yes, many of the depositions were conducted at the offices of the plaintiff companies that were claiming that NCW had engaged in illegal pricing policies, so we were out of town quite frequently.

Q: When you say we, who are you talking about?

A: The entire litigation team, which included myself, three partners, four associates, and several paralegals. We were all out of town at one point or another during this case.

Q: Does that include the defendant, Mr. Clark?

A: Yes, of course.

Q: Were you ever required to work closely with Mr. Clark?

A: Yes, as the senior associate on the case I met with him both on the road, and in Nita City quite frequently.

Q: When you were out of town, where would those meetings take place?

A: Well, in several cities we would use the office space of local counsel, but often times we would set up in Mr. Clark's hotel suite.

Q: During the work sessions in the hotel suite, were you and Mr. Clark ever alone?

A: Yes, that wasn't unusual, as we were often times the only two people on the team at some of the deposition sessions.

Q: At any of those times did Mr. Clark ever make a sexual advance towards you?

A: Yes, he did.

Q: When was the first time that happened?

A: It was well into the litigation, but I can't tell you when.

Q: Let me show you a document that we have marked as Exhibit 20, do you recognize that Exhibit?

A: Yes, it's my deposition.

Q: Directing your attention to Page 14, Lines 10-16, would you please read them to yourself?

A: Certainly.

Q: Have you finished reading that section of your deposition?

A: Yes.

Q: Taking from you Exhibit 20, do you now remember the first time that Mr. Clark made a sexual advance towards you during the NCW litigation?

A: Yes, it was in January of YR-3.

II

USE OF DEPOSITION AS PRIOR TESTIMONY

Federal Rule of Evidence 804

Direct Examination of Clifford Fuller by the Plaintiff:

Q: Was Michael DeAngelo considered for a partnership at P & G in June of YR-2?

A: He did come up that year but he put his decision over until the next year.

Q: How was that decision made?

A: I really can't be sure, today. I was mainly concerned with Ms. Polisi's case because, unlike Mr. DeAngelo, she decided to go forward in YR-2.

Assume that counsel attempted to refresh the memory of Mr. Fuller with the use of his deposition, but that attempt failed.

By Plaintiff's Counsel:

Your Honor, I move the admission of Exhibit 21, the deposition of Mr. Fuller, Page 86, Line 12 to the end of the page, and Page 87, Lines 1 through 22.

By Defendant's Counsel:

Objection, that's hearsay.

By Plaintiff's Counsel:

Your Honor, Mr. Fuller has testified to an incomplete memory of the reasons why Mr. DeAngelo was allowed to put his partnership decision at P & G over for one year from YR-2 to YR-1. He is therefore unavailable within the meaning of FRE 804(a)(3). This portion of his deposition, then, qualifies as former testimony pursuant to FRE 804(a)(1), an exception to the hearsay rule.

By the Court:

The exhibit will be received.

By Plaintiff's Counsel:

Your Honor, may I publish the exhibit by reading the questions asked by defendant's counsel at the deposition, and having the answers that Mr. Fuller gave at the time of his deposition read by him.

By the Court:

Go ahead.

NOTE: In the above scenario, counsel attempted to refresh the recollection of the witness before offering the deposition in evidence. This is the typical way in which counsel would proceed, but not required by the rules of evidence. In other words, there is no need to attempt to refresh a witness' recollection before introducing the deposition in this situation. The deposition could also have been offered pursuant to the Recorded Recollection exception to the hearsay rule pursuant to FRE 803(5). Former Testimony is the preferred exception to utilize because Recorded Recollections pursuant to FRE 803(5) may only be read to the jury, whereas Former Testimony pursuant to FRE 804(b)(1) may be received as a full exhibit.

The more typical use of the deposition as Former Testimony is when the witness is unavailable at all for trial testimony, and his or her entire testimony is presented to the trier of fact via the deposition. In these circumstances, depositions that are transcribed are normally published by counsel reading the questions, and someone playing the role of the unavailable witness reading the answers. Videotaped depositions are merely played for the jury.

III

<u>USE OF DEPOSITION FOR AN OFFER OF PROOF</u>

Federal Rule of Evidence 103

Cross Examination of Simon Clark by Plaintiff's Counsel:

Q: Ms. Polisi is not the first associate at Parker & Gould with whom you have had a sexual relationship, is she?

A: No

Q: In fact, your history of sexual relations with associates at Parker & Gould extends back over 10 years, doesn't it?

A: Well, my first relationship was over ten years ago, if that's what you mean.

Q: That's right sir, your first such relationship was over ten years ago, wasn't it?

A: That's right.

Q: All of those relationships ended, correct sir?

A: Obviously, yes.

Q: They all ended because you lied to those women, correct?

By Defendant's Counsel:

Objection. That question is argumentative and is attempt to assassinate the character of my client.

By Plaintiff's Counsel:

If I may be heard, your honor.

By the Court:

Please approach the Bench.

At Side Bar:

By Plaintiff's Counsel:

It is our position, your honor, that Mr. Clark was involved in numerous sexual relationships with associates at Parker & Gould and that each such relationship ended in some way, shape, manner, or form, when Mr. Clark promised to end his marriage, and reneged on that promise.

By the Court:

Do you have a basis for that allegation?

By Plaintiff's Counsel:

Yes your honor. If I can show to the court Exhibit 24, which is the deposition of Mr. Clark and refer you to the following pages and lines, you will see that my characterization is a correct statement of the facts of the case. Please refer to Page . . . .

IV

USE OF DEPOSITION AS A SOURCE FOR ADMISSIONS

Federal Rule of Evidence 801(d)(2)

Direct Examination of Mr. Fuller by Plaintiff's Counsel:

Q: Were you present at the meeting during which Ms. Polisi was considered for partnership at Parker & Gould?

A: Yes, I was there for the entire meeting.

Q: Why is it that Ms. Polisi was not made a partner at Parker and Gould?

A: There was no one reason I'm sure. A number of arguments both in favor and opposed to her candidacy were advanced.

Q: Was there a consideration of whether Mr. Clark would be comfortable having Ms. Polisi as a partner?

A: There were no arguments of that nature, but it may very well have been a consideration, after all Mr. Clark is and was and an important member of the firm in attracting clients.

By Defendant's Counsel:

Objection. Move to strike the answer as pure conjecture.

By Plaintiff's Counsel:

May I offer an Exhibit your honor?

By Defendant's Counsel:

May we approach your honor?

At Side Bar:

By Plaintiff's Counsel:

Your honor, if I may mark as Exhibit 25, the deposition of Ms. Jayne Post, who will be a witness in this case and who was at the time of this meeting, and remains a partner at Parker & Gould. I offer page 74, Lines 5–29, wherein Ms. Post says: "As between Ms. Polisi and Mr. Clark it was an easy question. Mr. Clark was a senior partner with the firm who generated a lot of business. Ms. Polisi, no matter what her talents, was never going to be as important to the firm as Mr. Clark. I'm sure a number of my partners considered those facts in the partnership decision . . . ." I am willing to withdraw my question to Mr. Fuller and publish this exhibit to the jury. Ms. Post is a partner at Parker and Gould and her statement in the deposition is admissible as an Admission pursuant to FRE 801(d)(2)(A).

By Defendant's Counsel:

Your honor, two points if I may. First, this statement by Ms. Post is an opinion and should not be admissible. Second, counsel has failed to offer the entirety of Ms. Post's statement on this subject pursuant to FRE 106. Her answer continues of Page 75, Lines 1-6, ". . . but they were in no way controlling to our decision at the meeting, and I certainly don't know of any effort on Mr. Clark's part to influence any of us against Ms. Polisi. He never even said that he would be uncomfortable working with Ms. Polisi if she were made a partner."

By the Court:

As to your first point, Admissions are not governed by the rules proscribing opinions. Your second point is well taken. The entirety of the statement should be read to the jury.

By Defendant's Counsel:

One other matter your honor. Ms. Post is certainly an agent of the defendant Parker & Gould, but she does not speak for Mr. Clark, in his role as an individual defendant in this case. I ask that you so instruct the jury pursuant to FRE 105.

By the Court:

I will so instruct the jury. Members of the jury . . .

* * *

While party admissions obtained during a deposition are useful at trial, and can be very effective in re-enforcing points to the jury during the examination of witnesses, the information obtained during deposition will also be the basis for dispositive motions in pretrial litigation. In addition, information obtained during depositions, is often used as a basis for F.R. Civ. P. Rule 36, Requests for Admission, which can also be utilized at trial, or as a means for narrowing the issues at trial.

V

USE OF DEPOSITION FOR IMPEACHMENT BY PRIOR INCONSISTENT STATEMENT

Federal Rules of Evidence 613 and 801(d)(1)

Cross Examination of Ms. Polisi by Defendant's Counsel:

Q: You ended your relationship with Mr. Clark in January of YR-2, didn't you?

A: Yes, he obviously wasn't interested in a serious relationship.

Q: I understand Ms. Polisi, but it was you who ended that relationship, right?

A: Right.

Q: Even though it was you who ended the relationship, you were unhappy about its ending, correct?

A: That's right.

Q: You were also ill during that period of time after the breakup, weren't you?

A: Yes. I was run down and I got a lot of colds.

Q: Your assignments fell of during that period, didn't they?

A: Yes.

Q: You were happy that you had less work to do, given your physical condition, weren't you?

A: No, I wanted the work, I just wasn't getting assignments.

Q: You weren't happy that you had less work to do?

A: No, I wanted to work.

Q: That hasn't always been your position has it, Ms. Polisi?

A: Of course it has, I was ready, willing and able to work.

Q: This isn't the first time you've given sworn testimony in this case, is it?

A: That's right I gave my deposition.

Q: And at that deposition you were present with your lawyer, correct?

A: Yes.

Q: And I was there?

A: Right.

Q: And there was a court reporter there, to take down everything you said, true?

A: True.

Q: And at that time I told you I was interested in finding out what you knew about the case we're trying here today, isn't that right?

A: I don't remember that, but I don't doubt you did.

Q: Nonetheless Ms. Polisi, before you answered my questions you swore to tell the truth, just like you did in court today. That's correct, isn't it?

A: Of course.

Q: After the deposition was over it was typed up and given to you to read and correct, wasn't it?

A: Yes.

Q: And you read and signed the deposition, didn't you?

A: I did.

Q: Now Ms. Polisi, are you sure that you weren't happy in the winter of YR-2, that you had less work to do?

A: Yes, I've answered your question.

Q: Ms. Polisi, let me show you what has been marked as Exhibit 20. Exhibit 20 is the deposition we've been talking about, isn't it?

A: Yes.

Q: Directing your attention to the last page, that's your signature, isn't it?

A: Yes, I signed the deposition.

Q: Turning to Page 24, Line 7, I asked you, "In light of your illness in the winter of YR-2, were you upset to receive fewer assignments than you had in the past?" That was my question wasn't it.

A: Yes.

Q: Your answer to that question appears at Line 10, doesn't it?

A: Yes.

Q: You answered by saying, "No, in fact, because I was ill, I was happy to have less work to do." That was your answer, wasn't it?

A: It appears so.

Q: You never complained to Mr. Clark, who was the head of the Litigation Section of the firm, about your assignments in the winter and spring of YR-2, did you?

A: No, under the circumstances, I did not.

Q: You also didn't complain to Mr. Fuller, who was Mr. Clark's Deputy, did you?

A: I believe I did say something to Cliff.

Q: In fact, Ms. Polisi, isn't it true that the only people you mentioned your lack of assignments to, before June of YR-2, were Mr. Hancock and Mr. DeAngelo, who were fellow associates at the firm, and your secretary, Ms. Gibson?

A: No, I'm sure I complained to Cliff and Simon's Administrative Aid, Ms. Jones, who was in charge of communicating assignments to the associates.

Q: Well Ms. Polisi, we discussed this very matter in your deposition that we talked about just a few minutes ago, didn't we?

A: I'm sure we did, but I don't recall it specifically.

Q: Let me show you Exhibit 20 again Ms. Polisi. At your deposition you swore to tell not only the truth, but the whole truth, isn't that right?

A: Right.

Q: I also told you that if you needed to complete an answer that you should just tell me, correct?

A: That's right.

Q: And each time we came back from a break I asked you if you wanted to change or add anything to your previous answers, right?

A: I believe you did.

Q: And when you read your deposition, you were instructed that you could correct or add to any answers to make them accurate, right?

A: Yes.

Q: Let me direct your attention to Page 90, Line 2 of your deposition. I asked you these questions and you gave these answers, and you correct me if I'm wrong. "Question: Before June of YR-2 when you were talking to Mr. Fuller about your partnership candidacy, who did you talk to about you lack of work assignments? Answer: Well I know I talked to my secretary. Question: Who else did you talk to about your lack of work assignments? Answer: I know I mentioned it to Mike DeAngelo. Question: Who else? Answer: Mark Hancock. Who else? Answer: That's all." Have I read those questions and answers correctly?

A: Yes, you have.

Q: So at your deposition the only people you claim you spoke to about your lack of work assignments, before June of YR-2, were your secretary, Mr. DeAngelo, and Mr. Hancock?

A: I guess so.

Q: You made no mention then of either Mr. Fuller or Ms. Jones?

A: Apparently not.

* * *

Counsel could now introduce the portions of the deposition referred to above, as extrinsic evidence of Polisi's inconsistent statement (for impeachment purposes) pursuant to FRE 613(b). These portions of the deposition are also admissible for the truth of their content because they are non-hearsay pursuant FRE 801(d)(1)(A) as inconsistent statements given under oath, or FRE 801(d)(2)(A) as party admissions.

WITNESS PREPARATION

By LOUIS M. NATALI, JR.
and ANTHONY J. BOCCHINO

These vignettes are designed to raise some of the ethical issues that arise in witness preparation for deposition testimony.

For the purposes of these vignettes assume that we are in the office of Polisi's lawyer on the day before her deposition is scheduled. Polisi and her lawyer have met many times before in the course of this litigation, and, to date, have developed an excellent working relationship.

<u>VIGNETTE ONE</u>

Lawyer:	Okay Maggie. Let's talk about some of the issues that might come up with respect to the problem of litigating your damages. You understand that whole rat's nest I'm sure.
Polisi:	Only too well. I'm really worried about this.
L:	Well, no need to worry, we'll work it out today. To help us work through the problems, why don't we role-play the deposition. Let's assume that I'm the law firm's lawyer and she asks you, "Tell me, by the way, how do you like being a law professor?"
P:	It's the greatest job in America, but don't tell anyone else. I've always wanted to teach, and I'm so happy to be out of the law practice rat race.
L:	That's your answer?
P:	Well yeah. You look like you just found out you had relatives on the *Titanic* or something. Did I say something wrong? What can I say, it's a great job.
L:	Well, let's say I'm a little surprised by your unguarded enthusiasm. It sounds like the firm did you a favor by firing you. But I want you to tell the truth. Perhaps it would sound better if you left out the opinions.

P: What do you mean? What opinions?

L: Well listen carefully to the question and just answer it directly. Do you enjoy your job?

P: Yes, it's a . . .

L: Yes answers the question. Anything more would be more than the question asks for, and likely to get into your opinion as to why the job is enjoyable or not.

P: I see. You know, I've given the same advice to my clients, but its easier said than done.

L: Right. Let's go on. What do you enjoy about your job?

P: The teaching, working with the students. I also like the research and writing, funny as that might seem.

L: Careful of the opinion. Your last comment was an opinion. Let's go on. So it's fair to say, then, that you enjoy your job?

P: Yes, that's fair.

L: Now Maggie. I'd prefer that you don't just agree with characterizations by the other lawyer. They will almost always lead to confusion. After that answer, they could argue that you are perfectly happy with your job and that can lessen your damages. Let's look and see if there isn't something about your job that you don't enjoy.

P: Okay, but it really is a good job.

L: Let's see how good. Do you enjoy earning a lot less money that you did with the firm?

P: No, of course not.

L: Do you miss the excitement of trial?

P: Sure.

L: Do you enjoy grading exams? No one enjoys grading exams.

P: You've got a point there.

L: How about faculty meetings? I've heard they can be ponderous.

P: That is true. The arguments seem to repeat themselves and do seem to always fill the allotted time.

L: How do you feel about the tenure treadmill? Isn't the publish or perish problem stressful? Do you enjoy that aspect of your new career?

P: I guess you're right. I like the research and writing, but it's very frustrating when I find that what were original thoughts for me turn out to be similar to something else already in print, or when I find that I just wasn't as focused as I need to be. My colleagues are good about it, but I do feel the stress to publish in order to be successful.

L: What else is less than perfect?

P: Now that you mention it, it can get pretty lonely. I like my colleagues, but they have their own projects. I sometimes feel closed off from the real world excitement of law practice. But all in all I like my job. Especially the freedom I have to pursue my own intellectual interests, and I love to have some free time to spend with kids.

L: You see what I mean Maggie. It's true that you have a good job. But there is some downside that has to be explained, and there are also some things that you miss about the practice of law. Your answers need to be balanced.

P: You're right. Thanks. That's very helpful.

L: That's why you hired me. Now, let's try again. Tell me about your job as a law professor?

P: What do you want to know?

L: Do you like it?

P: There are things I like about it and things I don't.

L: What do you like?

P: Teaching, working with students, the freedom to pursue intellectual goals.

L: What don't you like?

P: Grading exams, some faculty meetings, the lower salary. It's sometimes a pretty solitary existence. Not like the excitement of working on a big case. Also, the publish or perish aspect of the scholarship requirements of the job can be stressful.

L: Okay. Let's stop there. That was much better. It was much more factual. I like the way you made me ask a more direct question. Keep that up. Again, and you were doing very well, avoid giving conclusions.

P: But what if they ask for my opinion. Aren't they entitled to that?

L: They can ask for your opinion, but you don't have to give one. If you prefer not to opine or guess, say so. If they insist, just be careful that it's clear that you are just giving an opinion or guessing, whatever the case might be.

End of Transcript

VIGNETTE TWO

L: Now let's look at questions about your career goals as they existed while you were at the law firm. Was it always your eventual goal to teach?

P: Yes, but much later after I had saved enough money to pay for the education of my kids, including graduate school if they wanted, and saved for my retirement.

L: Great, but suppose she asks, "Wasn't it your ultimate goal to teach in a law school?"

P: I'll tell her, "Sure I wanted to teach but I loved working on the kind of cases I was assigned to at P & G. That is, before Clark black-balled me at the firm. I don't know now what I would have done and when. It's all speculation. It would be very hard for me to go back to work in a law firm now after what Clark did to me. He and P & G have really soured me, by what they did to me, toward law practice. They treated me despicably." How's that. Does that tell them what you want them to hear?

L: Well I don't know. Let's talk about it a little. Don't you think you're laying it on a little thick?

P: I don't think so. Whenever I start to talk about this I get really angry. Those SOB's had no right to do to me what they did.

L: I understand, but . . .

P: But what. They deserve to hear what they did to me in no uncertain terms and so does the judge and jury. There was nothing nice about what they did.

L: Well, I don't know. We need to discuss this. You don't want to come off like you're hysterical. Why don't we see whether we can separate the truth from the anger?

P: That will be a challenge, but I'm game if you are.

L: I think it's real important to your case Maggie, so let's get at it.

End of Transcript

LEGAL ETHICS

By ANTHONY J. BOCCHINO

Legal Ethics—Vignette I

Professional Responsibilities Issues
in Interviewing the Former Employee
of an Opposing Party

Assume for the purposes of this Vignette that Mary Jones is a friend of Maggie Polisi's and that Polisi has asked her to represent Polisi in a potential law suit against Simon Clark and P & G arising out of her discharge by the firm. Polisi has given Jones the name of Cliff Fuller as a potential witness for her. Jones has learned from Polisi that Fuller was the Deputy Chief of the Litigation Section at P & G during the time in which she was denied partnership. Polisi has also informed Jones that Fuller was a mentor to her at the firm and that she and Fuller remain on friendly terms. Jones has also learned that Fuller has recently left P & G to become Vice President and General Counsel of Nita Computer World. Polisi has arranged for Jones and Fuller to meet at a local restaurant. Jones has not spoken to Fuller before the meeting date. For the purposes of this Vignette, refer to Pennsylvania Rules of Professional Conduct, Rules 4.1–4.4, (attached) which are consistent with the ABA Model Rules of Professional Conduct.

A. The meeting is scheduled for after normal work hours (8 P.M.). Jones has not informed anyone at P & G of her intent to meet with Fuller. Is the meeting under those circumstances ethically permissible?

The following occurs at the meeting where Jones, Polisi and Fuller are present:

Polisi:	Cliff, this is my friend, Mary Jones. As you know she's giving me some advice on what I should do about losing my job.
Fuller:	Nice to meet you, Mary.
Jones:	You too, Mr. Fuller.
Fuller:	Call me Cliff.
Jones:	Alright, Cliff. I want to thank you for meeting with me. Your help is very important. Maggie tells me that you were one of her mentors at P & G. Is that right?

Fuller:	Of course.
Jones:	Well I'd like to get your insight into what happened if I could. When did you and Maggie first work together at P & G?

B.   Based on the above, does Jones have any ethical problems in continuing her interview of Fuller?

Assume now that Jones has filed suit against Clark and P & G on the basis of gender discrimination and that she has the same information about Fuller as above, with the addition that she has been informed that Fuller was a partner at P & G and the Deputy Chair of the Litigation Section at P & G during the time in which Polisi was considered for and denied partnership in the firm.

C.   May Jones talk to Fuller about the law suit without informing opposing counsel? What must Jones say to or ask Fuller before interviewing him about the law suit on behalf of her client?

End of Vignette

Legal Ethics—Vignette II

Assume that you are the lawyer for the law firm of Parker & Gould. The firm has been served with a copy of the Polisi's complaint against the firm and Simon Clark. As counsel for P & G you need to speak with Clark to obtain from him his response to the other members of the firm, and they confirm that it was common knowledge within the firm that Clark and Polisi were romantically involved and that some time in YR-2 that the relationship ended. Every partner has denied that the termination of the affair between Polisi and Clark had anything to do with the firm's decision not to offer a partnership to Polisi.

The management committee of P & G has told you of their preference that Clark and P & G run a joint defense. Their view is that separate counsel would give the impression that the firm believed that Clark had acted improperly. They have also told you that the reality of the situation is that Clark is very important to the firm as a "rainmaker" for the Litigation Section, and they don't wish to antagonize him.

You have called Clark and asked for an appointment with him to discuss the case. He has informed you that he does not have separate counsel, that he assumed that the firm would undertake his representation in this case which he considers to be frivolous. For purposes of this Vignette, please refer to Pennsylvania Rules of Professional Conduct, Rules 1.6, 1.7, 1.9, 1.10, and 1.16 (attached) which are consistent with the ABA Model Rules of Professional Conduct.

A.   May you meet with Clark and find out his position on the allegations by the Plaintiff? If so, what must you tell him about your position within the law suit?

Assume that during the interview with Clark, Clark admits to having sexual relationships with other employees of P & G in the past. All of the people whose names he volunteer are no longer with the firm, and all of them left after their sexual relationship with Clark ended. Clark maintains that their leaving P & G and the end of their relationships with him are not related. In response to your questions, Clark admits that he had a sexual relationship with a woman associate, who after the end of the relationship went on to become a partner in the firm, but he refuses to disclose her name to you.

B.   Does this information create any problems in your representing both Clark and P & G?

Later in the interview, Clark tells you that he never asked anyone in the firm to vote against Polisi's partnership application. He says, however, that he doesn't doubt that there might be some partners in the Litigation Section who voted against her candidacy in an effort to please him.

C.   Does this information create any problems in representing both Clark and P & G?

Finally, at one juncture in the interview, Clark says to you that he would like to "speak frankly" with you. After you assure he should be candid, Clark tells you that contrary to what he had told you earlier that in the heat of the moment, when Polisi ended their relationship, that he said something like "You're all the same. You don't know when you have a good thing going. You're going to regret this." He states, however, that he was speaking about personal, and not professional regret.

D.   Does this information create any problems in representing both Clark and P & G? If so, what must you do?

End of Vignette

Legal Ethics—Vignette III

Assume that you are the counsel for P & G. The Plaintiff has noticed the deposition of Mary Jones, the administrative assistant to Simon Clark. Her responsibilities included (during the period of time during which Clark was the Chair of the Litigation Section) the administrative assignment of associates to cases when requests for assistance were received from partners.

MODEL RULES OF PROFESSIONAL CONDUCT

RULE 1.6   Confidentiality of Information[*]

(a) A lawyer shall not reveal information relating to representation of a client unless the client consents after consultation, except for disclosures that are impliedly authorized in order to carry out the representation, and except as stated in paragraph (b).

(b) A lawyer may reveal such information to the extent the lawyer reasonably believes necessary:

(1) to prevent the client from committing a criminal act that the lawyer believes is likely to result in imminent death or substantial bodily harm; or

(2) to establish a claim or defense on behalf of the lawyer in a controversy between the lawyer and the client, to establish a defense to a criminal charge or civil claim against the lawyer based upon conduct in which the client was involved, or to respond to allegations in any proceeding concerning the lawyer's representation of the client.

'Editors' Note: As previously proposed by the Kutak Commission, Rules 1.6 (Revised Final Draft, June 30, 1982) read as follows: RULE 1.6 Confidentiality of Information (a) A lawyer shall not reveal information relating to representation of a client unless the client consents after consultation, except for disclosures that are impliedly authorized in order to carry out the representation, and except as stated in paragraph (b).

(b) A lawyer may reveal such information to the extent the lawyer reasonably believes necessary:

(1) to prevent the client from committing a criminal or fraudulent act that the lawyer reasonably believes is likely to result in death or substantial bodily harm, or in substantial injury to the financial interests or property of another;

(2) to rectify the consequences of a client's criminal or fraudulent act in the furtherance of which the lawyer's services had been used;

(3) to establish a claim or defense on behalf of the lawyer in a controversy between the lawyer and the client, or to establish a defense to a criminal charge, civil claim or disciplinary complaint against the lawyer based upon conduct in which the client was involved; or

(4) to comply with other law.

In 1991, the ABA House of Delegates again rejected a proposal from its ethics committee to amend Rule 1.6(b) to add the rectification language found in subsection (b)(2) of the 1982 Revised Final Draft. As of the end of 1991, about a third of the states have adopted a rectification provision.

Please see: State by State Analysis of Ethics Rules on Client Confidences, reprinted after these Model Rules.

COMMENT

[1] The lawyer is part of a judicial system charged with upholding the law. One of the lawyer's functions is to advise clients so that they avoid any violation of the law in the proper exercise of their rights.

[2] The observance of the ethical obligation of a lawyer to hold inviolate confidential information of the client not only facilitates the full development of facts essential to proper representation of the client but also encourages people to seek early legal assistance.

[3] Almost without exception, clients come to lawyers in order to determine what their rights are and what is, in the maze of laws and regulations, deemed to be legal and correct. The common law recognizes that the client's confidences must be protected from disclosures. Based upon experience, lawyers know that almost all clients follow the advise given, and the law is upheld.

[4] A fundamental principle in the client-lawyer relationship is that the lawyer maintain confidentiality of information relating to the representation. The client is thereby encouraged to communicate fully and frankly with the lawyer even as to embarrassing or legally damaging subject matter.

[5] The principle of confidentiality is given effect in two related bodies of law, the attorney-client privilege (which includes the work product doctrine) in the law of evidence and the rule of confidentiality established in professional ethics. The attorney-client privilege applies in judicial and other proceedings in which a lawyer may be called as a witness or otherwise required to produce evidence concerning a client. The rule of client-lawyer confidentiality applies in situations other than those where evidence is sought from the lawyer through compulsion of law. The confidentiality rule applies not merely to matters communicated in confidence by the client but also to all information relating to the representation, whatever its source. A lawyer may not disclose such information except as authorized or required by the Rules of Professional Conduct or other law. See also Scope.

[6] The requirement of maintaining confidentiality of information relating to representation applies to government lawyers who may disagree with the policy goals that their representation is designed to advance.

Authorized Disclosure

[7] A lawyer is impliedly authorized to make disclosures about a client when appropriate in carrying out the representation, except to the extent that the client's instructions or special circumstances limit that authority. In litigation, for example, a lawyer may disclose information by admitting a fact that cannot properly be disputed, or in negotiation by making a disclosure that facilitates a satisfactory conclusion.

[8] Lawyers in a firm may, in the course of the firm's practice, disclose to each other information relating to a client of the firm, unless the client has instructed that particular information be confined to specified lawyers.

Disclosure Adverse to Client

[9] The confidentiality rule is subject to limited exceptions. In becoming privy to information about a client, a lawyer may foresee that the client intends serious harm to another person. However, to the extent a lawyer is required or permitted to disclose a client's purposes, the client will be inhibited from revealing facts which would enable the lawyer to counsel against a wrongful course of action. The public is better protected if full and open communication by the client is encouraged than if it is inhibited.

[10] Several situations must be distinguished. First, the lawyer may not counsel or assist a client in conduct that is criminal or fraudulent. See Rule 1.2(d). Similarly, a lawyer has a duty under Rule 3.3(a)(4) not to use false evidence. This duty is essentially a special instance of the duty prescribed in Rule 1.2(d) to avoid assisting a client in criminal or fraudulent conduct.

[11] Second, the lawyer may have been innocently involved in past conduct by the client that was criminal or fraudulent. In such a situation the lawyer has not violated Rule 1.2(d), because to "counsel or assist" criminal or fraudulent conduct requires knowing that the conduct is of that character.

[12] Third, the lawyer may learn that a client intends prospective conduct that is criminal and likely to result in imminent death or substantial bodily harm. As stated in paragraph, (b)(1), the lawyer has professional discretion to reveal information in order to prevent such consequences. The lawyer may make a disclosure in order to prevent homicide or serious bodily injury which the lawyer reasonably believes is intended by a client. It is very difficult for a lawyer to "know" when such a heinous purpose will actually be carried out, for the client may have a change of mind.

[13] The lawyer's exercise of discretion requires consideration of such factors as the nature of the lawyer's relationship with the client and with those who might be injured by the client, the lawyer's own involvement in the transaction and factors that may extenuate the conduct in question. Where practical, the lawyer should seek to persuade the client to take suitable action. In any case, a disclosure adverse to the client's interest should be no greater than the lawyer reasonably believes necessary to the purpose. A lawyer's decision not to take preventive action permitted by paragraph (b)(1) does not violate this Rule.

Withdrawal

[14] If the lawyer's services will be used by the client in materially furthering a course of criminal or fraudulent conduct, the lawyer must withdraw, as stated in Rule 1.16(a)(1).

[15] After withdrawal the lawyer is required to refrain from making disclosure of the clients' confidences, except as otherwise provided in Rule 1.6. Neither this Rule nor Rule 1.8(b) nor Rule 1.16(d) prevents the lawyer from giving notice of the fact of withdrawal, and the lawyer may also withdraw or disaffirm any opinion, document, affirmation, or the like.

[16]   Where the client is an organization, the lawyer may be in doubt whether contemplated conduct will actually be carried out by the organization. Where necessary to guide conduct in connection with this Rule, the lawyer may make inquiry within the organization as indicated in Rule 1.13(b).

Dispute Concerning Lawyer's Conduct

[17]   Where a legal claim or disciplinary charge alleges complicity of the lawyer in a client's conduct or other misconduct of the lawyer involving representation of the client, the lawyer may respond to the extent the lawyer reasonably believes necessary to establish a defense. The same is true with respect to a claim involving the conduct or representation of a former client. The lawyer's right to respond arises when an assertion of such complicity has been made. Paragraph (b)(2) does not require the lawyer to await the commencement of an action or proceeding that charges such complicity, so that the defense may be established by responding directly to a third party who has made such an assertion. The right to defend, of course, applies where a proceeding has been commenced. Where practicable and not prejudicial to the lawyer's ability to establish the defense, the lawyer should advise the client of the third party's assertion and request that the client respond appropriately. In any event, disclosure should be no greater than the lawyer reasonably believes is necessary to vindicate innocence, the disclosure should be made in a manner which limits access to the information to the tribunal or other persons having a need to know it, and appropriate protective orders or other arrangements should be sought by the lawyer to the fullest extent practicable.

[18]   If the lawyer is charged with wrongdoing in which the client's conduct is implicated, the rule of confidentiality should not prevent the lawyer from defending against the charge. Such a charge can arise in a civil, criminal or professional disciplinary proceeding, and can be based on a wrong allegedly committed by the lawyer against the client, or on a wrong alleged by a third person; for example, a person claiming to have been defrauded by the lawyer and client acting together. A lawyer entitled to a fee is permitted by paragraph (b)(2) to prove the services rendered in an action to collect it. This aspect of the rule expresses the principle that the beneficiary of a fiduciary relationship may not exploit it to the detriment of the fiduciary. As stated above, the lawyer must make every effort practicable to avoid unnecessary disclosure of information relating to a representation, to limit disclosure to those having the need to know it, and to obtain protective orders or make other arrangements minimizing the risk of disclosure.

Disclosures Otherwise Required or Authorized

[19] The attorney-client privilege is differently defined in various jurisdictions. If a lawyer is called as a witness to give testimony concerning a client, absent waiver by the client, Rule 1.6(a) requires the lawyer to invoke the privilege when it is applicable. The lawyer must comply with the final orders of a court or other tribunal of competent jurisdiction requiring the lawyer to give information about the client.

[20] The Rules of Professional Conduct in various circumstances permit or require a lawyer to disclose information relating to the representation. See Rules 2.2, 2.3, 3.3, and 4.1. In addition to these provisions, a lawyer may be obligated or permitted by other provisions of law to give information about a client. Whether another provision of law supersedes Rules 1.6 is a matter of interpretation beyond the scope of these Rules, but a presumption should exist against such a supersession.

Former Client

[21] The duty of confidentiality continues after the client-lawyer relationship has terminated.

MODEL CODE COMPARISON

[1] Rule 1.6 eliminates the two-pronged duty under the Model Code in favor of a single standard protecting all information about a client "relating to the representation." Under DR 4-101, the requirement applied only to information protected by the attorney-client privilege and to information "gained in" the professional relationship that "the client has requested be held inviolate or the disclosure of which would be embarrassing or would be likely to be detrimental to the client." EC 4-4 added that the duty differed from the evidentiary privilege in that it existed "without regard to the nature or source of information or the fact that others share the knowledge." Rule 1.6 imposes confidentiality on information relating to the representation even if it is acquired before or after the relationship existed. It does not require the client to indicate information that is to be confidential, or permit the lawyer to speculate whether particular information might be embarrassing or detrimental.

[2] Paragraph (a) permits a lawyer to disclose information where impliedly authorized to do so in order to carry out the representation. Under DR 4-101(B) and (C), a lawyer was not permitted to reveal "confidences" unless the client first consented after disclosure.

[3] Paragraph (b) redefines the exceptions to the requirement of confidentiality. Regarding paragraph (b)(1), DR-101(C)(3) provided that a lawyer "may reveal . . . [t]he intention of his client to commit a crime and the information necessary to prevent the crime." This option existed regardless of the seriousness of the proposed crime.

[4] With regard to paragraph (b)(2), DR 4-101(C)(4) provided that a lawyer may reveal "[c]onfidences or secrets necessary to establish or collect his fee or to defend himself or his employers or associates against an accusation or wrongful conduct." Paragraph (b)(2) enlarges the exception to include disclosure of information relating to claims by the lawyer other than for the lawyer's fee; for example, recovery of property from the client.

RULE 1.7 Conflict of Interest: General Rule

(a) A lawyer shall not represent a client if the representation of that client will be directly adverse to another client, unless:

(1) the lawyer reasonably believes the representation will not adversely affect the relationship with the other client; and

(2) each client consents after consultation.

(b) A lawyer shall not represent a client if the representation of that client may be materially limited by the lawyer's responsibilities to another client or to a third person, or by the lawyer's own interests, unless:

(1) the lawyer reasonably believes the representation will not be adversely affected; and

(2) the client consents after consultation. When representation of multiple clients in a single matter is undertaken, the consultation shall include explanation of the implications of the common representation and the advantages and risks involved.

COMMENT
Loyalty to a Client

[1] Loyalty is an essential element in the lawyer's relationship to a client. An impermissible conflict of interest may exist before representation is undertaken, in which event the representation should be declined. The lawyer should adopin both litigation and non-litigation matters the parties and issues involved and to determine whether there are actual or potential conflicts of interest.

[2] If such a conflict arises after representation has been undertaken, the lawyer should withdraw from the representation. See Rule 1.16. Where more than one client is involved and the lawyer withdraws because a conflict arises after representation, whether the lawyer may continue to represent any of the clients is determined by Rule 1.9. See also Rule 2.2(c). As to whether a client-lawyer relationship exists or, having once been established, is continuing, seet reasonable procedures, appropriate for the size and type of firm and practice, to determine Comment to Rule 1.3 and Scope.

[3] As a general proposition, loyalty to a client prohibits undertaking representation directly adverse to that client without that client's consent. Paragraph (a) applies only when the representation of one client would be directly adverse to the other.

[4] Loyalty to a client is also impaired when a lawyer cannot consider, recommend or carry out an appropriate course of action for the client because of the lawyer's other responsibilities or interests. The conflict in effect forecloses alternatives that would otherwise be available to the client. Paragraph (b) addresses such situations. A possible conflict does not itself preclude the representation. The critical questions are the likelihood that a conflict will

eventuate and, if it does, whether it will materially interfere with the lawyer's independent professional judgment in considering alternatives or foreclose courses of action that reasonably should be pursued on behalf of the client. Consideration should be given to whether the client wishes to accommodate the other interest involved.

Consultation and Consent

[5] A client may consent to representation notwithstanding a conflict. However, as indicated in paragraph (a)(1) with respect to representation directly adverse to a client, and paragraph (b)(1) with respect to material limitations on representation of a client, when a disinterested lawyer would conclude that the client should not agree to the representation under the circumstances, the lawyer involved cannot properly ask for such agreement or provide representation on the basis of the client's consent. When more than one client is involved, the question of conflict must be resolved as to each client. Moreover, there may be circumstances where it is impossible to make the disclosure necessary to obtain consent. For example, when the lawyer represents different clients in related matters and one of the clients refuses to consent to the disclosure necessary to permit the other client to make an informed decision, the lawyer cannot properly ask the latter to consent.

Lawyer's Interests

[6] The lawyer's own interests should not be permitted to have adverse effect on representation of a client. For example, a lawyer's need for income should not lead the lawyer to undertake matters that cannot be handled competently and at a reasonable fee. See Rules 1.1 and 1.5. If the probity of a lawyer's own conduct in a transaction is in serious question, it may be difficult or impossible for the lawyer to give a client detached advice. A lawyer may not allow related business interests to affect representation, for example, by referring clients to an enterprise in which the lawyer has an undisclosed interest.

Conflicts in Litigation

[7] Paragraph (a) prohibits representation of opposing parties in litigation. Simultaneous representation of parties whose interests in litigation may conflict, such as co-plaintiffs or co-defendants, is governed by paragraph (b). An impermissible conflict may exist by reason of substantial discrepancy in the parties' testimony, incompatibility in position in relation to an opposing party or the fact that there are substantially different possibilities of settlement of the claims or liabilities in question. Such conflicts can arise in criminal cases as well as civil. The potential for conflict of interest in representing multiple defendants in a criminal case is so grave that ordinarily a lawyer should decline to represent more than one co-defendant. On the other hand, common representation of persons having similar interest is proper if the risk of adverse effect is minimal and the requirements of paragraph (b) are met. Compare Rule 2.2 involving intermediation between clients.

[8] Ordinarily, a lawyer may not act as advocate against a client the lawyer represents in some other matter, even if the other matter is wholly unrelated. However, there are circumstances in which a lawyer may act as advocate against a client. For example, a lawyer representing an enterprise with diverse operations may accept employment as an advocate against the enterprise in an unrelated matter if doing so will not adversely affect the lawyer's relationship with the enterprise or conduct of the suit and if both clients consent upon consultation. By the same token, government lawyers in some circumstances may represent government employees in proceedings in which a government agency is the opposing party. The propriety of concurrent representation can depend on the nature of the litigation. For example, a suit charging fraud entails conflict to a degree not involved in a suit for a declaratory judgment concerning statutory interpretation.

[9] A lawyer may represent parties having antagonistic position on a legal question that has arisen in different cases, unless representation of either client would be adversely affected. Thus, it is ordinarily not improper to assert such positions in cases pending in different trial courts, but it may be improper to do so in cases pending at the same time in an appellate court.

Interest of Person Paying for a Lawyer's Service

[10] A lawyer may be paid from a source other than the client, if the client is informed of that fact and consents and the arrangement does not compromise the lawyer's duty of loyalty to the client. See Rule 1.8(f). For example, when an insurer and its insured have conflicting interest in a matter arising from a liability insurance agreement, and the insurer is required to provide special counsel for the insured, the arrangement should assure the special counsel's professional independence. So also, when a corporation and its directors or employees are involved in a controversy in which they have conflicting interest, the corporation may provide funds for separate legal representation of the directors or employees, if the clients consent after consultation and the arrangement ensures the lawyer's professional independence.

Other Conflict Situations

[11] Conflicts of interest in contexts other than litigation sometimes may be difficult to assess. Relevant factors in determining whether there is potential for adverse effect include the duration and intimacy of the lawyer's relationship with the client or clients involved, the functions being performed by the lawyer, the likelihood that actual conflict will arise, and the likely prejudice to the client from the conflict if it does arise. The question is often one of proximity and degree.

[12] For example, a lawyer may not represent multiple parties in a negotiation whose interests are fundamentally antagonistic to each other, but common representation is permissible where the clients are generally aligned in interest even though there is some difference of interest among them.

[13] Conflict questions may also arise in estate planning and estate administration. A lawyer may be called upon to prepare wills for several family members, such as husband and wife, and, depending upon the circumstances, a conflict of interest may arise. In estate administration the identity of the client may be unclear under the law of a particular jurisdiction. Under one view, the client is the fiduciary; under another view the client is the estate or trust, including its beneficiaries. The lawyer should make clear the relationship to the parties involved.

[14] A lawyer for a corporation or other organization who is also a member of its board of directors should determine whether the responsibilities of the two roles may conflict. The lawyer may be called on to advise the corporation in matters involving actions of the directors. Consideration should be given to the frequency with which such situation may arise, the potential intensity of the conflict, the effect of the lawyer's resignation from the board, and the possibility of the corporation's obtaining legal advice from another lawyer in such situations. If there is material risk that the dual role will compromise the lawyer's independence of professional judgement, the lawyer should not serve as a director.

Conflict Charged by an Opposing Party

[15] Resolving questions of conflict of interest is primarily the responsibility of the lawyer undertaking the representation. In litigation, a court may raise the question when there is reason to infer that the lawyer has neglected the responsibility. In a criminal case, inquiry by the court is generally required when a lawyer represents multiple defendants. Where the conflict is such as clearly to call in question the fair or efficient administration of justice, opposing counsel may properly raise the question. Such an objection should be viewed with caution, however, for it can be misused as a technique of harassment. See Scope.

MODEL CODE COMPARISON

[1] DR 5-101(A) provided that "[e]xcept with the consent of his client after full disclosure, a lawyer shall not accept employment if the exercise of his professional judgment on behalf of the client will be or reasonably may be affected by his own financial, business, property, or personal interests." DR 5-105(A) provided that a lawyer "shall decline proffered employment if the exercise of his independent professional judgment in behalf of a client will be or is likely to be adversely affected by the acceptance of the proffered employment, or if it would be likely to involve him in representing differing interests, except to the extent permitted under DR 5-105(C)." DR 5-105(C) provided that "a lawyer may represent multiple clients if it is obvious that he can adequately represent the interest of each and if each consents to the representation after full disclosure of the possible effect of such representation on the exercise of his independent professional judgment on behalf on each." DR 5-107(B) provided that a lawyer "shall not permit a person who recommends, employs, or pays him to render legal services for another to direct or regulate his professional judgment in rendering such services."

[2] Rule 1.7 clarifies DR 5-105(A) by requiring that, when the lawyer's other interests are involved, not only must the client consent after consultation but also that, independent of such consent, the representation reasonably appears not to be adversely affected by the lawyer's other interests. This requirement appears to be the intended meaning of the provision in DR 5-105(C) that "it is obvious that he can adequately represent" the client, and was implicit in EC 5-2, which stated that a lawyer "should not accept proffered employment if his personal interests or desires will, or there is a reasonable possibility that they will, affect adversely the advice to be given or services to be rendered the prospective client."

RULE 1.8 Conflict of Interests: Prohibited Transactions

(a) A lawyer shall not enter into a business transaction with a client or knowingly acquire an ownership, possessory, security or other pecuniary interest adverse to a client unless:

(1) the transaction and terms on which the lawyer acquires the interest are fair and reasonable to the client and are fully disclosed and transmitted in writing to the client in a manner which can be reasonably understood by the client;

(2) the client is given a reasonable opportunity to seek the advice of independent counsel in the transaction; and

(3) the client consents in writing thereto.

(b) A lawyer shall not use information relating to representation of a client to the disadvantage of the client unless the client consents after consultation, except as permitted or required by Rule 1.6 or Rule 3.3.

(c) A lawyer shall not prepare an instrument giving the lawyer or a person related to the lawyer as parent, child, sibling, or spouse any substantial gift from a client, including a testamentary gift, except where the client is related to the donee.

(d) Prior to the conclusion of representation of a client, a lawyer shall not make or negotiate an agreement giving the lawyer literary or media rights to a portrayal or account based in substantial part on information relating to the representation.

(e) A lawyer shall not provide financial assistance to a client in connection with pending or contemplated litigation, except that:

(1) a lawyer may advance court costs and expenses of litigation, the repayment of which may be contingent on the outcome of the matter; and

(2) a lawyer representing a indigent client may pay court costs and expenses of litigation on behalf of the client.

(f) A lawyer shall not accept compensation for representing a client form on other than the client unless:

(1) the client consents after consultation;

(2) there is no interference with the lawyer's independence of professional judgment or with the client-lawyer relationship; and

(3) information relating to representation of a client is protected as required by Rule 1.6.

(g) A lawyer who represents two or more clients shall not participate in making an aggregate settlement of the claims of or against the clients, or in a criminal case an aggregated agreement as to guilty or nolo contendere pleas, unless each client consents after consultation, including disclosure of the existence and nature of all the claims or pleas involved and of the participation of each person in the settlement.

(h) A lawyer shall not make an agreement prospectively limiting the lawyer's liability to a client for malpractice unless permitted by law and the client is independently represented in making the agreement, or settle a claim for such liability with an unrepresented client or former client without first advising that person in writing that independent representation is appropriate in connection therewith.

(i) A lawyer related to another lawyer as parent, child, sibling or spouse shall not represent a client in a representation directly adverse to a person whom the lawyer knows is represented by the other lawyer except upon consent by the client after consultation regarding the relationship.

(j) A lawyer shall not acquire a proprietary interest in the cause of action or subject matter of litigation the lawyer is conducting for a client, except that the lawyer may:

(1) acquire a lien granted by law to secure the lawyer's fee or expenses; and

(2) contract with a client for a reasonable contingent fee in a civil case.

RULE 1.9 Conflict of Interest: Former Client

(a) A lawyer who has formerly represented a client in a matter shall not thereafter represent another person in the same or a substantially related matter in which that person's interests are materially adverse to the interests of the former client unless the former client consents after consultation.

(b) A lawyer shall not knowingly represent a person in the same or a substantially related matter in which a firm with which the lawyer formerly was associated had previously represented a client

(1) whose interests are materially adverse to that person; and

(2) about whom the lawyer had acquired information protected by Rules 1.6 and 1.9 (c) that is material to the matter; unless the former client consents after consultation.

(c) A lawyer who had formerly represented a client in a matter or whose present or former firm has formerly represented a client in a matter shall not thereafter:

(1) use information relating to the representation to the disadvantage of the former client except as Rule 1.6 or Rule 3.3 would permit or require with respect to a client, or when the information has become generally known; or

(2) reveal information relating to the representation except as Rule 1.6 or Rule 3.3 would permit or require with respect to a client.

COMMENT

[1] After termination of a client-lawyer relationship, a lawyer may not represent another client except in conformity with this Rule. The principles in Rule 1.7 determine whether the interests of the present and former client are adverse. Thus, a lawyer could not properly seek to rescind on behalf of a new client a contract drafted on behalf of the former client.

* * *

Lawyers Moving Between Firms

[5] The other rubric formerly used for dealing with disqualification is the appearance or impropriety proscribed in Canon 9 of the ABA Model Code of Professional Responsibility. This rubric has a two-fold problem. First, the appearance of impropriety can be taken to include any new client-lawyer relationship that might make a former client feel anxious. If that meaning were adopted, disqualification would become little more than a question of subjective judgment by the former client. Second, since "impropriety" is undefined, the term "appearance of impropriety" is question-begging. It therefore has to be recognized that the problem of disqualification cannot be properly resolved either by simple analogy to a lawyer practicing alone or by the very general concept of appearance of impropriety.

[6] A rule based on a functional analysis is more appropriate for determining the question of disqualification. Two functions are involved: preserving confidentiality and avoiding positions adverse to a client.

Confidentiality

[7] Preserving confidentiality is a question of access to information. Access to information, in turn, is essentially a question of fact in particular circumstances, aided by inferences, deductions or working presumptions that reasonably may be made about the way in which lawyers work together. A lawyer may have general access to files of all clients of a law firm and may regularly participate in discussions of their affairs; it should be inferred that such a lawyer in fact is privy to all information about all the firm's clients. In contrast, another lawyer may have access to the files of only a limited number of clients and participate in discussion of the affairs of no other clients; in the absence of information to the contrary, it should be inferred that such a lawyer in fact is privy to information about the clients actually served but not those of other clients.

[8] Application of paragraph (b) depends on a situation's particular facts. In such an inquiry, the burden of proof should rest upon the firm whose disqualification is sought.

[9] Paragraph (b) operates to disqualify the lawyer only when the lawyer involved has actual knowledge of information protected by Rules 1.6 and 1.9(b). Thus, if a lawyer while with on firm acquired no knowledge or information relating to a particular client of the firm, and that lawyer later joined another firm, neither the lawyer individually nor the second firm is disqualified from representing another client in the same or a related matter even though the interests of the two clients conflict. See Rule 1.10(b) for the restrictions on a firm once a lawyer has terminated association with the firm.

[10]   Independent of the question of disqualification of a firm, a lawyer changing professional association has a continuing duty to preserve confidentiality of information about a client formerly represented. See Rules 1.6 and 1.9.

RULE 1.10 Imputed Disqualification: General Rule

(a) While lawyers are associated in a firm, none of them shall knowingly represent a client when any one of them practicing alone would be prohibited from doing so by Rules 1.7, 1.8(c), 1.9, or 2.2.

(b) When a lawyer has terminated an association with a firm, the firm is not prohibited from thereafter representing a person with interests materially adverse to those of a client represented by the formerly associated lawyer and not currently represented by the firm, unless

(1) the matter is the same or substantially related to that in which the formerly associated lawyer represented the client; and

(2) any lawyer remaining in the firm has information protected by Rules 1.6 and 1.9(c) that is material to the matter.

(c) A disqualification prescribed by this rule may be waived by the affected client under the conditions stated in Rule 1.7.

COMMENT
Definition of "Firm"

[1] For purposes of the Rules of Professional Conduct, the term "firm" includes lawyers in a private firm, and lawyers in the legal department of a corporation or other organization, or in a legal services organization. Whether two or more lawyers constitute a firm within this definition can depend on the specific facts. For example, two practitioners who share office space and occasionally consult or assist each other ordinarily would not be regarded as constituting a firm. However, if they present themselves to the public in a way suggesting that they are a firm or conduct themselves as a firm, they should be regarded as a firm for the purposes of the Rules. The terms of any formal agreement between associated lawyers are relevant in determining whether they are a firm, as is the fact that they have mutual access to information concerning the clients they serve. Furthermore, it is relevant in doubtful cases to consider the underlying purpose of the Rule that is involved. A group of lawyers could be regarded as a firm for purposes of the rule that the same lawyer should not represent opposing parties in litigation, while it might not be so regarded for purposes of the rule that information acquired by one lawyer is attributed to the other.

[2] With respect to the law department of an organization, there is ordinarily no question that the members of the department constitute a firm within the meaning of the Rules of Professional Conduct. However, there can be uncertainty as to the identity of the client. For example, it may not be clear whether the law department of a corporation represents a subsidiary or an affiliated corporation, as well as the corporation by which the members of the department are directly employed. A similar question can arise concerning an unincorporated association and its local affiliates.

[3] Similar questions can also arise with respect to lawyers in legal aid. Lawyers employed in the same unit of a legal service organization constitute a firm, but not necessarily those employed in separate units. As in the case of independent practitioners, whether the lawyers should be treated as associated with each other can depend on the particular rule that is involved, and on the specific facts of the situation.

[4] Where a lawyer has joined a private firm after having represented the government, the situation is governed by Rule 1.11(a) and (b); where a lawyer represents the government after having served private clients, the situation is governed by Rule 1.11(c)(1). The individual lawyer involved is bound by the Rules generally, including Rules 1.6, 1.7, and 1.9.

[5] Different provisions are thus made for movement of a lawyer from one private firm to another and for movement of a lawyer between a private firm and the government. The government is entitled to protection of its client confidences and, therefore, to the protections provided in Rules 1.6, 1.9, and 1.11. However, if the more extensive disqualification in Rule 1.10 were applied to former government lawyers, the potential effect on the government would be unduly burdensome. The government deals with all private citizens and organizations and, thus, has a much wider circle of adverse legal interests than does any private law firm. In these circumstances, the government's recruitment of lawyers would be seriously impaired if Rule 1.10 were applied to the government. On balance, therefore, the government is better served in the long run by the protections stated in Rule 1.11.

Principles of Imputed Disqualification

[6] The rule of imputed disqualification stated in paragraph (a) gives effect to the principle of loyalty to the client as it applies to lawyers who practice in a law firm. Such situations can be considered from the premise that a firm of lawyers is essentially one lawyer for purposes of the rules governing loyalty to the client, or from the premise that each lawyer is vicariously bound by the obligation of loyalty owed by each lawyer with whom the lawyer is associated. Paragraph (a) operates only among the lawyers currently associated in a firm. When a lawyer moves from one firm to another, the situation is governed by Rules 1.9(b) and 1.10(b).

[7] Rule 1.10(b) operates to permit a law firm, under certain circumstances, to represent a person with interests directly adverse to those of a client represented by a lawyer who formerly was associated with the firm. The Rule applies regardless of when the formerly associated lawyer represented the client. However, the law firm may not represent a person with interests adverse to those of a present client of the firm, which would violate Rule 1.7. Moreover, the firm may not represent a person where the matter is the same or substantially related to that in which the

formerly associated lawyer represented the client and any other lawyer currently in the firm has material information protected by Rules 1.6 and 1.9(c).

MODEL CODE COMPARISON

DR 5-105(D) provided that "[i]f a lawyer is required to decline or to withdraw from employment under a Disciplinary Rule, no partner, or associate, or any other lawyer affiliated with him or his firm, may accept or continue such employment."

RULE 1.16 Declining or Terminating Representation

(a) Except as stated in paragraph (c), a lawyer shall not represent a client or, where representation has commenced, shall withdraw from the representation of a client if:

(1) the representation will result in violation of the rules of professional conduct or law;

(2) the lawyer's physical or mental condition materially impairs the lawyer's ability to represent the client; or

(3) the lawyer is discharged.

(b) Except as stated in paragraph (c), a lawyer may withdraw from representing a client if withdrawal can be accomplished without material adverse effect on the interests of the client, or if:

(1) the client persists in a course of action involving the lawyer's services that the lawyer reasonably believes is criminal or fraudulent;

(2) the client has used the lawyer's services to perpetrate a crime or fraud;

(3) a client insists upon pursuing an objective that the lawyer considers repugnant or imprudent;

(4) the client fails substantially to fulfill an obligation to the lawyer regarding the lawyer's services and has been given reasonable warning that the lawyer will withdraw unless the obligation is fulfilled;

(5) the representation will result in an unreasonable financial burden on the lawyer or has been rendered unreasonably difficult by the client; or

(6) other good cause for withdrawal exists.

(c) When ordered to do so by a tribunal, a lawyer shall continue representation notwithstanding good cause for terminating the representation.

(d) Upon termination of representation, a lawyer shall take steps to the extent reasonably practicable to protect a client's interests, such as giving reasonable notice to the client, allowing time for employment of other counsel, surrendering papers and property to which the client is entitled and refunding any advance payment of fee that has not been earned. The lawyer may retain papers relating to the client to the extent permitted by other law.

COMMENT

[1] A lawyer should not accept representation in a matter unless it can be performed competently, promptly, without improper conflict of interest, and to completion.

Mandatory Withdrawal

[2] A lawyer ordinarily must decline or withdraw from representation if the client demands that the lawyer engage in conduct that is illegal or violates the Rules of Professional Conduct or other law. The lawyer is not obliged to decline or withdraw simply because the client suggests such a course of conduct; a client may make such a suggestion in the hope that a lawyer will not be constrained by a professional obligation.

[3] When a lawyer has been appointed to represent a client, withdrawal ordinarily requires approval of the appointing authority. See also Rule 6.2. Difficulty may be encountered if withdrawal is based on the client's demand that the lawyer engage in unprofessional conduct. The court may wish an explanation for the withdrawal, while the lawyer may be bound to keep confidential the facts that would constitute such an explanation. The lawyer's statement that professional considerations require termination of the representation ordinarily should be accepted as sufficient.

Discharge

[4] A client has a right to discharge a lawyer at any time, with or without cause, subject to liability for payment for the lawyer's services. Where future dispute about the withdrawal may be anticipated, it may be advisable to prepare a written statement reciting the circumstances.

[5] Whether a client can discharge appointed counsel may depend on applicable law. A client seeking to do so should be given a full explanation of the consequences. These consequences may include a decision by the appointing authority that appointment of successor counsel is unjustified, thus requiring the client to represent himself.

[6] If the client is mentally incompetent, the client may lack the legal capacity to discharge the lawyer, and in any event the discharge may be seriously adverse to the client's interests. The lawyer should make special effort to help the client consider the consequences and, in an extreme case, may initiate proceedings for a conservatorship or similar protection of the client. See Rule 1.14.

Optional Withdrawal

[7] A lawyer may withdraw from representation in some circumstances. The lawyer has the option to withdraw if it can be accomplished without material adverse effect on the client's interests. Withdrawal is also justified if the client persists in a course of action that the lawyer reasonably believes is criminal or fraudulent, for a lawyer is not required to be associated with such conduct even if the lawyer does not further it. Withdrawal is also permitted if the lawyer's services were misused in the past even if that would materially prejudice the client. The lawyer also may withdraw where the client insists on a repugnant or imprudent objective.

[8] A lawyer may withdraw if the client refuses to abide by the terms of an agreement relating to the representation, such as an agreement concerning fees or court costs or an agreement limiting the objectives of the representation.

Assisting the Client Upon Withdrawal

[9] Even if the lawyer has been unfairly discharged by the client, a lawyer must take all reasonable steps to mitigate the consequences to the client. The lawyer may retain papers as security for a fee only to the extent permitted by law.

[10] Whether or not a lawyer for an organization may under certain unusual circumstances have a legal obligation to the organization after withdrawing or being discharged by the organization's highest authority is beyond the scope of these Rules.

MODEL CODE COMPARISON

[1] With regard to paragraph (a), DR 2-109(A) provided that a lawyer "shall not accept employment . . . if he knows or it is obvious that (the prospective client) wishes to . . . (b)ring a legal action . . . or otherwise have steps taken for him, merely for the purpose of harassing or maliciously injuring any person . . ." Nor may a lawyer accept employment if the lawyer is aware that the prospective client wishes to "(p)resent a claim or defense . . . that is not warranted under existing law, unless it can be supported by good faith argument for an extension, modification, or reversal of existing law." DR 2-110(B) provided that a lawyer "shall withdraw from employment . . . if:

"(1) He knows or it is obvious that his client is bringing the legal action . . . or is otherwise having steps taken for him, merely for the purpose of harassing or maliciously injuring any person.

RULE 3.3 Candor Toward the Tribunal

(a) A lawyer shall not knowingly:

(1) make a false statement of material fact or law to a tribunal;

(2) fail to disclose a material fact to a tribunal when disclosure is necessary to avoid assisting a criminal or fraudulent act by the client;

(3) fail to disclose to the tribunal legal authority in the controlling jurisdiction known to the lawyer to be directly adverse to the position of the client and not disclosed by opposing counsel; or

(4) offer evidence that the lawyer knows to be false. If a lawyer has offered material evidence and comes to know of its falsity, the lawyer shall take reasonable remedial measures.

(b) The duties stated in paragraph (a) continue to the conclusion of the proceeding, and apply even if compliance requires disclosure of information otherwise protected by Rule 1.6.

(c) A lawyer may refuse to offer evidence that the lawyer reasonably believes is false.

(d) In an ex parte proceeding, a lawyer shall inform the tribunal of all material facts known to the lawyer which will enable the tribunal to make an informed decision, whether or not the facts are adverse.

COMMENT

[1] The advocate's task is to present the client's case with persuasive force. Performance of that duty while maintaining confidences of the client is qualified by the advocate's duty of candor to the tribunal. However, an advocate does not vouch for the evidence submitted in a cause; the tribunal is responsible for assessing its probative value.

Representations by a Lawyer

[2] An advocate is responsible for pleadings and other documents prepared for litigation, but is usually not required to have personal knowledge of matters asserted therein, for litigation documents ordinarily present assertions by the client, or by someone on the client's behalf, and not assertions by the lawyer. Compare Rule 3.1. However, an assertion purporting to be on the lawyer's own knowledge, as in an affidavit by the lawyer or in a statement in open court, may properly be made only when the lawyer knows the assertion is true or believes it to be true on the basis of a reasonably diligent inquiry. There are circumstances where failure to make a disclosure is the equivalent of an affirmative misrepresentation. The obligation prescribed in Rule 1.2(d) not to counsel a client to commit or assist the client in committing a fraud applies in litigation. Regarding compliance with rule 1.2(d), see the Comment to that Rule. See also the Comment to Rule 8.4(b).

Misleading Legal Argument

[3] Legal argument based on a knowingly false representation of law constitutes dishonesty toward the tribunal. A lawyer is not required to make a disinterested exposition of the law, but must recognize the existence of pertinent legal authorities. Furthermore, as stated in paragraph (a)(3), an advocate has a duty to disclose directly adverse authority in the controlling jurisdiction which has not been disclosed by the opposing party. The underlying concept is that legal argument is a discussion seeking to determine the legal premises properly applicable to the case.

False Evidence

[4] When evidence that a lawyer knows to be false is provided by a person who is not the client, the lawyer must refuse to offer it regardless of the client's wishes.

[5] When false evidence is offered by the client, however, a conflict may arise between the lawyer's duty to keep the client's revelations confidential and the duty of candor to the court.

Upon ascertaining that material evidence is false, the lawyer should seek to persuade the client that the evidence should not be offered or, if it has been offered, that its false character should immediately be disclosed. If the persuasion is ineffective, the lawyer must take reasonable remedial measures.

[6] Except in the defense of a criminal accused, the rule generally recognized is that, if necessary to rectify the situation, an advocate must disclose the existence of the client's deception to the court or to the other party. Such a disclosure can result in grave consequences to the client, including not only a sense of betrayal but also loss of the case and perhaps a prosecution for perjury. But the alternative is that the lawyer cooperate in deceiving the court, thereby subverting the truth-finding process which the adversary system is designed to implement. See Rule 1.2(d). Furthermore, unless it is clearly understood that the lawyer will act upon the duty to disclose the existence of false evidence, the client can simply reject the lawyer's advice to reveal the false evidence and insist that the lawyer keep silent. Thus, the client could in effect coerce the lawyer into being a party to fraud on the court.

Perjury by a Criminal Defendant

[7] Whether an advocate for a criminally accused has the same duty of disclosure has been intensely debated. While it is agreed that the lawyer should seek to persuade the client to refrain from perjurious testimony, there has been dispute concerning the lawyer's duty when that persuasion fails. If the confrontation with the client occurs before trial, the lawyer ordinarily can withdraw. Withdrawal before trial may not be possible, however, either because trial is imminent, or because the confrontation with the client does not take place until the trial itself, or because no other counsel is available.

[8] The most difficult situation, therefore, arises in a criminal case where the accused insists on testifying when the lawyer knows that the testimony is perjurious. The lawyer's effort to rectify the situation can increase the likelihood of the client's being convicted as well as opening the possibility of a prosecution for perjury. On the other hand, if the lawyer does not exercise control over the proof, the lawyer participates, although in a merely passive way, in deception of the court.

[9] Three resolutions of this dilemma have been proposed. One is to permit the accused to testify by a narrative without guidance through the lawyer's questioning. This compromises both contending principles; it exempts the lawyer from the duty to disclose false evidence but subjects the client to an implicit disclosure of information imparted to counsel. Another suggested resolution, of relatively recent origin, is that the advocate be entirely excused from the duty to reveal perjury if the perjury is that of the client. This is a coherent solution but makes the advocate a knowing instrument of perjury.

[10] The other resolution of the dilemma is that the lawyer must reveal the client's perjury if necessary to rectify the situation. A criminal accused has a right to the assistance of

an advocate, a right to testify, and a right of confidential communication with counsel. However an accused should not have a right to assistance of counsel in committing perjury. Furthermore, an advocate has an obligation, not only in professional ethics but under the law as well, to avoid implication in the commission of perjury or other falsification of evidence. See Rule 1.2(d).

Remedial Measures

[11] If perjured testimony or false evidence has been offered, the advocate's proper course ordinarily is to remonstrate with the client confidentially. If that fails, the advocate should seek to withdraw if that will remedy the situation. If withdrawal will not remedy the situation or is impossible, the advocate should make disclosure to the court. It is for the court then to determine what should be done—making a statement about the matter to the trier of fact, ordering a mistrial, or perhaps nothing. If the false testimony was that of the client, the client may controvert the lawyer's version of their communication when the lawyer discloses the situation to the court. If there is an issue whether the client has committed perjury, the lawyer cannot represent the client in resolution of the issue and a mistrial may be unavoidable. An unscrupulous client might in this way attempt to produce a series of mistrials and thus escape prosecution. However, a second such encounter could be construed as a deliberate abuse of the right to counsel and as such a waiver of the right to further representation.

Constitutional Requirements

[12] The general rule—that an advocate must disclose the existence of perjury with respect to a material fact, even that of a client—applies to defense counsel in criminal cases, as well as in other instances. However, the definition of the lawyer's ethical duty in such a situation may be qualified by constitutional provisions for due process and the right to counsel in criminal cases. In some jurisdictions these provisions have been construed to require that counsel present an accused as a witness if the accused wishes to testify, even if counsel knows the testimony will be false. The obligation of the advocate under these Rules is subordinate to such a constitutional requirement.

Duration of Obligation

[13] A practical time limit on the obligation to rectify the presentation of false evidence has to be established. The conclusion of the proceeding is a reasonably definite point for the termination of the obligation.

Refusing to Offer Proof Believed to Be False

[14] Generally speaking, a lawyer has authority to refuse to offer testimony or other proof that the lawyer believes is untrustworthy. Offering such proof may reflect adversely on the lawyer's ability to discriminate in the quality of evidence and thus impair the lawyer's

effectiveness as an advocate. In criminal cases, however, a lawyer may, in some jurisdictions, be denied this authority by constitutional requirements governing the right to counsel.

Ex Parte Proceedings

[15] Ordinarily, an advocate has the limited responsibility of presenting one side of the matters that a tribunal should consider in reaching a decision; the conflicting position is expected to be presented by the opposing party. However, in an ex parte proceeding, such as an application for a temporary restraining order, there is no balance of presentation by opposing advocates. The object of an ex parte proceeding is nevertheless to yield a substantially just result. The judge has an affirmative responsibility to accord the absent party just consideration. The lawyer for the represented party has the correlative duty to make disclosures of material facts known to the lawyer and that the lawyer reasonably believes are necessary to an informed decision.

MODEL CODE COMPARISON

(1) Paragraph (a)(1) is substantially identical to DR 7-102(A)(5), which provided that a lawyer shall not "knowingly make a false statement of law or fact."

(2) Paragraph (a)(2) is implicit in DR 7-102(A)(3), which provided that "a lawyer shall not . . . knowingly fail to disclose that which he is required by law to reveal."

(3) Paragraph (a)(3) is substantially identical to DR 7-106(B)(1).

(4) With regard to paragraph (a)(4), the first sentence of this subparagraph is similar to DR 7-102(A)(4), which provided that a lawyer shall not "knowingly use" perjured testimony or false evidence. The second sentence of paragraph (a)(4) resolves an ambiguity in the Model Code concerning the action required of a lawyer who discovers that the lawyer has offered perjured testimony or false evidence. DR 7-102(A)(4), quoted above, did not expressly deal with this situation, but the prohibition against "use" of false evidence can be construed to preclude carrying through with a case based on such evidence when that fact has become known during the trial. DR 7-102(B)(1), also noted in connection with Rule 1.6, provided that a lawyer "who receives information clearly establishing that . . . his client has . . . perpetrated a fraud upon . . . a tribunal shall if the client does not rectify the situation . . . reveal the fraud to the . . . tribunal . . ." Since use of perjured testimony or false evidence is usually regarded as "fraud" upon the court, DR 7-102(B)(1) apparently required disclosure by the lawyer in such circumstances. However, some states have amended DR 7-102(B)(1) in conformity with an ABA-recommended amendment to provide that the duty of disclosure does not apply when the "information is protected as a privileged communication." This qualification may be empty, for the rule of attorney-client privilege has been construed to exclude communications that further a crime, including the crime of perjury. On this interpretation of DR 7-102(B)(1), the lawyer has a duty to disclose the perjury.

(5) Paragraph (c) confers discretion on the lawyer to refuse to offer evidence that he "reasonably believes: is false. This gives the lawyer more latitude than DR 7-102(A)(4), which prohibited the lawyer from offering evidence the lawyer "knows" is false.

(6) There was no counterpart in the Model Code to paragraph (d).

RULE 3.4 Fairness to Opposing Party and Counsel

A lawyer shall not:

(a) unlawfully obstruct another party's access to evidence or unlawfully alter, destroy or conceal a document or other material having potential evidentiary value. A lawyer shall not counsel or assist another person to do any such act;

(b) falsify evidence, counsel or assist a witness to testify falsely, or offer an inducement to a witness that is prohibited by law;

(c) knowingly disobey an obligation under the rules of a tribunal except for an open refusal based on an assertion that no valid obligation exists;

(d) in pretrial procedure, make a frivolous discovery request or fail to make reasonably diligent effort to comply with a legally proper discovery request by an opposing party;

(e) in trial, allude to any matter that the lawyer does not reasonably believe is relevant or that will not be supported by admissible evidence, assert personal knowledge of facts in issue except when testifying as a witness, state a personal opinion as to the justness of a cause, the credibility of a witness, the culpability of a civil litigant or the guilt or innocence of an accused; or

(f) request a person other than a client to refrain from voluntarily giving relevant information to another party unless:

(1) the person is a relative or an employee or other agent of a client; and

(2) the lawyer reasonably believes that the person's interests will not be adversely affected by refraining from giving such information.

COMMENT

[1] The procedure of the adversary system contemplates that the evidence in a case is to be marshalled competitively by the contending parties. Fair competition in the adversary system is secured by prohibitions against destruction or concealment of evidence, improperly influencing witnesses, obstructive tactics in discovery procedure, and the like.

[2] Documents and other items of evidence are often essential to establish a claim or defense. Subject to evidentiary privileges, the right of an opposing party, including the government, to obtain evidence through discovery or subpoena is an important procedural right. The exercise of that right can be frustrated if relevant material is altered, concealed or destroyed. Applicable law in many jurisdictions makes it an offense to destroy material for purpose of impairing its availability in a pending proceeding or one whose commencement can be foreseen. Falsifying evidence is also generally a criminal offense. Paragraph (a) applies to evidentiary material generally, including computerized information.

[3] With regard to paragraph (b), it is not improper to pay a witness's expenses or to compensate an expert witness on terms permitted by law. The common law rule in most jurisdictions is that it is improper to pay an occurrence witness any fee for testifying and that it is improper to pay an expert witness a contingent fee.

[4] Paragraph (f) permits a lawyer to advise employees of a client to refrain from giving information to another party, for the employees may identify their interests with those of the client. See also Rule 4.2.

RULE 4.1 Truthfulness in Statements to Others

In the course of representing a client a lawyer shall not knowingly:

(a) make a false statement of material fact or law to a third person; or

(b) fail to disclose a material fact to a third person when disclosure is necessary to avoid assisting a criminal or fraudulent act by a client, unless disclosure is prohibited by Rule 1.6.

COMMENT
Misrepresentation

[1] A lawyer is required to be truthful when dealing with others on a client's behalf, but generally has no affirmative duty to inform an opposing party of relevant facts. A misrepresentation can occur if the lawyer incorporates or affirms a statement of another person that the lawyer knows is false. Misrepresentations can also occur by failure to act.

Statements of Fact

[2] This Rule refers to statements of fact. Whether a particular statement should be regarded as one of fact can depend on the circumstances. Under generally accepted conventions in negotiation, certain types of statements ordinarily are not taken as statements of material fact. Estimates of price or value placed on the subject of a transaction and a party's intentions as to an acceptable settlement of a claim are in this category, and so is the existence of an undisclosed principal except where nondisclosure of the principal would constitute fraud.

Fraud by Client

[3] Paragraph (b) recognizes that substantive law may request a lawyer to disclose certain information to avoid being deemed to have assisted the client's crime or fraud. The requirement of disclosure created by this paragraph is, however, subject to the obligations created by Rule 1.6.

MODEL CODE COMPARISON

(1) Paragraph (a) is substantially similar to DR 7-102(A)(5), which stated that "(i)n his representation of a client, a lawyer shall not . . . (k)nowingly make a false statement of law or fact."

(2) With regard to paragraph (b), DR 7-102(A)(3) provided that a lawyer shall not "(c)onceal or knowingly fail to disclose that which he is required by law to reveal."

RULE 4.2 Communication With Person Represented by Counsel

In representing a client, a lawyer shall not communicate about the subject of the representation with a party the lawyer knows to be represented by another lawyer in the matter, unless the lawyer has the consent of the other lawyer or is authorized by law to do so.

COMMENT

[1] This Rule does not prohibit communication with a party, or an employee or agent of a party, concerning matters outside the representation. For example, the existence of a controversy between a government agency and a private party, or between two organization, does not prohibit a lawyer for either from communicating with nonlawyer representatives of the other regarding a separate matter. Also, parties to a matter may communicate directly with each other and a lawyer having independent justification for directly with each other and a lawyer having independent justification for directly with each other and a lawyer having independent justification for communicating with the other party is permitted to do so. Communications authorized by law include, for example, the right of a party to a controversy with a government agency to speak with government officials about the matter.

[2] In the case of an organization, this Rule prohibits communications by a lawyer for one party concerning the matter in representation with persons having a managerial responsibility on behalf of the organization, and with any other person whose act or omission in connection with that matter may be imputed to the organization for purposes of civil or criminal liability or whose statement may constitute an admission on the part of the organization. If an agent or employee of the organization is represented in the matter by his or her own counsel, the consent by that counsel to a communication will be sufficient for purposes of this Rule. Compare Rule 3.4(f). This Rule also covers any person, whether or not a party to a formal proceeding, who is represented by counsel concerning the matter in question.

RULE 4.4 Respect for Rights of Third Persons

In representing a client, a lawyer shall not use means that have no substantial purpose other than to embarrass, delay, or burden a third person, or use methods of obtaining evidence that violate the legal rights of such a person.

MODEL CODE COMPARISON

This Rule is substantially identical to DR 7-104(A)(1).

RULE 4.3 Dealing With Unrepresented Person

In dealing on behalf of a client with a person who is not represented by counsel, a lawyer shall not state or imply that the lawyer is disinterested. When the lawyer knows or reasonably should know that the unrepresented person misunderstands the lawyer's role in the matter, the lawyer shall make reasonable efforts to correct the misunderstanding.

COMMENT

An unrepresented person, particularly one not experienced in dealing with legal matters, might assume that a lawyer is disinterested in loyalties or is a disinterested authority on the law even when the lawyer represents a client. During the course of a lawyer's representation of a client, the lawyer should not give advice to an unrepresented person other than the advice to obtain counsel.

MODEL CODE COMPARISON

There is no direct counterpart to this Rule in the Model code. DR 7-104(a)(2) provided that a lawyer shall not "[g]ive advice to a person who is not represented by a lawyer, other than the advice to secure counsel . . ."

PROBLEMS IN DEALING WITH OPPOSING COUNSEL AT DEPOSITION

Prepared by **ANTHONY J. BOCCHINO**
and **LOUIS M. NATALI, JR.**

PART ONE—*THE INTERFERING LAWYER*
DEPOSITION OF MARGARET POLISI

By Ms. Smith:

Q: When was the first time that you worked for Mr. Clark as an Associate?

By Ms. Jones: Objection as to form. You may answer.

A: I can't be certain, but probably in my first year as an Associate.

Q: Would that have been in the fall of your first year or later?

By Ms. Jones: Objection as to form. You may answer.

A: I think it would have been in the fall, there was a case involving the same bank, Nita City Trust, that was the client in a case I worked as a paralegal, and Mr. Clark asked me to work on the new case right after I started with the firm.

Q: How long did the case last?

By Ms. Jones: Objection as to form. You may answer.

A: I only did some research work, so not very long in terms of my personal involvement.

Q: Well, how long did the case itself last?

By Ms. Jones: Oh counselor, what possible relevance can that have to this case, the witness said that she only did research on the case. At this rate this is going to take forever. Answer the question Ms. Polisi. But counselor, can't we move on to something of more relevance to this law suit?

By Ms. Smith: I'll ask whatever I like. Obviously your client's relationship with Mr. Clark, in the work place and otherwise, is at the heart of this claim and any case she and Clark worked on together is relevant. I ask you again Ms. Polisi, how long did the case you and Mr. Clark worked on in your first year as an Associate last?

By Ms. Jones: Objection as to form. You may answer.

A: I really don't know for sure, I wasn't involved.

By Ms. Jones: See counselor. Now that you've obtained that earth shattering information can we move on to something more relevant to this case. I need to inform you that we need to be done with this by 5:30 this afternoon.

By Ms. Smith: We'll finish when we finish. Let's move on to something else.

....

PART TWO—*THE TESTIFYING LAWYER*

DEPOSITION OF MARGARET POLISI

By Ms. Smith:

Q: Ms. Polisi, you've testified that you first worked with Mr. Clark as an associate in the fall of your first year in that position. When was the next time you worked on a case for Mr. Clark as an Associate?

By Ms. Jones: Excuse me counsel, do you mean actually work with him in person, or merely work on a case that he was in charge of. I think you'll find the answers might be different. But go ahead and answer the question Maggie, if you understand it.

A: I'm not sure I understand the question.

Q: What don't you understand?

By Ms. Jones: I've already explained the ambiguity.

By Ms. Smith: Answer my question Ms. Polisi. What don't you understand?

A: I worked on a number of cases on which Mr. Clark was the lead counsel in my first and second years with the firm as an associate, but I did not actually work with him personally on those cases.

Q: Well, how many cases did you work on that were headed up by Mr. Clark during your first two years as an associate in any manner?

By Ms. Jones: If you can remember at this time.

A: I don't really remember.

Q: Was it more than five?

By Ms. Jones: Counselor, she said she didn't remember. Answer the question if you can Ms. Polisi.

A: I don't remember the number, but probably . . .

By Ms. Jones: Don't guess, only if you know.

A: I don't know.

PART THREE - *THE CONFERRING LAWYER*
DEPOSITION OF MARGARET POLISI

By Ms. Smith:

Q: How frequently was your work as an associate evaluated at Parker & Gould?

A: I'm not sure what you mean by that.

By Ms. Jones: Excuse me counsel, we need to talk.

(After approximately 30 seconds)

By Ms. Jones: Excuse me counsel, go ahead.

By Ms. Smith:

Q: What didn't you understand about my last question?

A: Well, we received feedback on our work all the time, but there was only one formal evaluation each year. For me it was in September, which was my anniversary date.

Q: Let me show you what has been marked as Exhibit 3A which appears to me a memo to the "M. Polisi File" dated September 10, YR-10. Do you . . . .

By Ms. Jones: Just a moment counsel, we need to look at that Exhibit together.

(After approximately a minute of reading and whispered conversation)

A: I never saw this at the time it was made. I only saw it after it was produced in discovery. I can't be sure if it's accurate about what was said to me, if that's what you're driving at. It's been so long. But the grade is what they gave me in the first year.

By Ms. Smith:

Q: What else can you tell me about that evaluation?

By Ms. Jones: Excuse me again, counsel.

(After approximately 30 seconds of whispered conversation)

A: That's all, but as I said, I don't know if the rest of that exhibit, other than the grade and the raise, is accurate as to what was said to me at that evaluation by Mr. Milton.

PART FOUR—*THE INSTRUCTING LAWYER*
DEPOSITION OF SIMON CLARK

By Ms. Jones:

Q: Mr. Clark, we're now back from our lunch break. Is there anything that happened over the lunch break that will keep you from giving full and complete testimony?

A: No.

Q: Would you like to change or expand upon any of your answers from this morning?

A: No.

Q: All right Mr. Clark. When was the first time that you had a sexual relationship with any employee at Parker & Gould?

A: I don't remember.

Q: Was it more than 10 years ago.

By Ms. Smith: The witness said he doesn't remember. Don't speculate Mr. Clark.

By Ms. Jones: I need to get a time frame on this counsel. Was it over 10 years ago, Mr. Clark, that you had your first sexual relationship with an employee of Parker & Gould?

By Ms. Smith: He's told you he doesn't remember. Don't answer the question Mr. Clark.

By Ms. Jones: All right. When was the first sexual relationship that you had with an employee at Parker & Gould that you do remember?

A: I can't give you a date. I just don't recall.

Q: Can you recall a name?

By Ms. Smith: That's vague. Don't answer the question.

By Ms. Jones: Given that you can't recall the names of any employees at P & G with whom you've had a sexual relationship or the dates, are you denying that any such relationships existed?

By Ms. Smith: Assumes a fact not in evidence.

By Ms. Jones: Answer the question, sir.

By Ms. Smith: No, don't answer the question in that form. It assumes a fact not in evidence.

By Ms. Jones: Are you instructing the witness not to answer?

By Ms. Smith: I'm instructing the witness not to answer a question that assumes a fact not in evidence, and therefore would create an unclear and inaccurate record. Just rephrase your question and he'll be happy to answer it.

By Ms. Jones: Are you refusing to answer the question based on counsel's instruction, Mr. Clark?

By Ms. Smith: I'll not allow him to answer any question that will create a mistaken impression of the facts of this case.

By Ms. Jones: Mr. Clark, have you ever had a sexual relationship with anyone other than your wife whose name you can recall?

By Ms. Smith: That's outrageous counsel, don't answer that question. It's way beyond the permissible scope of this deposition.

ATTACHMENT TO PROBLEMS IN DEALING WITH OPPOSING COUNSEL

FRCP 30(d)(1) provides:

Any objection to evidence during a deposition shall be stated concisely and in a non-argumentative and non-suggestive manner. A party may instruct a deponent not to answer only when necessary to preserve a privilege, to enforce a limitation on evidence directed by the court, or to present a motion under paragraph (3).

FRCP 30(d)(3) provides in part:

At any time during the deposition, on motion of a party or of the deponent and upon a showing that the examination is being conducted in bad faith or in such manner as unreasonably to annoy, embarrass, or oppress the deponent or party, the court . . . may order the officer conducting the examination to cease forthwith from taking the deposition, or may limit the scope and manner of the taking of the deposition. . . .

Arthur J. HALL, Plaintiff,

v.

CLIFTON PRECISION, A DIVISION OF LITTON SYSTEMS, INC.
Civ. A. No. 92-5947.

United States District Court,

E.D. Pennsylvania.

July 29, 1993.

Civil action was commenced. During discovery, dispute arose regarding conduct of deposition. The District Court, Gawthrop, J., held that: (1) witness being deposed and his or her attorney may not confer during course of deposition unless conference is for purpose of determining whether privilege should be asserted, and (2) witness and counsel are not entitled to confer about document shown to witness during deposition before witness answers questions about it.

Ordered accordingly.

Robert F. Stewart, Philadelphia, PA, for defendant.

Joel W. Todd, Philadelphia, PA, for plaintiff.

OPINION

GAWTHROP, District Judge.

Currently at bar is an issue on which, despite its presence in nearly every case brought under the Federal Rules of Civil Procedure, there is not a lot of caselaw: the conduct of lawyers at depositions. More specifically, the questions before the court are (1) to what extent may a lawyer confer with a client, off the record and outside earshot of the other lawyers, during a deposition of the client, and (2) does a lawyer have the right to inspect, before the deposition of a client begins, all documents which opposing counsel intends to show the client during the deposition, so that the lawyer can review them with the client before the deposition?

In this case, Robert F. Stewart, Esquire, counsel for defendant, noticed the deposition of the plaintiff, Arthur J. Hall. Before the deposition began, Mr. Hall's counsel, Joel W. Todd, Esquire, asked Mr. Stewart for a copy of each document which Mr. Stewart intended to show Mr. Hall during the deposition so that he could review the documents with Mr. Hall before the deposition began. Mr. Stewart declined to produce the documents.

At the beginning of the deposition, Mr. Stewart described the deposition process to Mr. Hall. During that description, he told Mr. Hall, "[c]ertainly ask me to clarify any question that you do not understand. Or if you have any difficulty understanding my questions, I'll be happy to try to rephrase them to make it possible for you to be able to answer them." Deposition of

Arthur J. Hall, at 5-6. Mr. Todd then interjected, "Mr. Hall, at any time if you want to stop and talk to me, all you have to do is indicate that to me." Id. at 6. Mr. Stewart then stated his position: "[t]his witness is here to give testimony, to be answering my questions, and not to have conferences with counsel in order to aid him in developing his responses to my questions." Id.

During the brief, unfinished deposition, there were two interruptions. The first occurred when, according to Mr. Todd, Mr. Hall wished to confer with him about the meaning of the word "document." Nevertheless, when the deposition resumed, Mr. Hall asked Mr. Stewart about the meaning of "document." Id. at 9-10. The second interruption occurred when Mr. Stewart showed a document to Mr. Hall and began to ask him a question about it. Before Mr. Stewart finished his question about the document, Mr. Todd said, "I've got to review it with my client." Id. at 18. Mr. Stewart stated his objection "to Mr. Todd reviewing with his client documents that Mr. Hall is about to be questioned on in this deposition." Id. The parties then contacted the court, which ordered that the deposition be adjourned until the question of attorney-client discussion during the deposition could be resolved. That afternoon, the court held a conference with both counsel about their conduct at the deposition. At the conference, Mr. Todd asserted that an attorney and client have the right to confer with one another at any time during the taking of the client's deposition. At the end of the conference, the court requested counsel to submit letter briefs on the issue, which they have done.

The Federal Rules of Civil Procedure give the court control over the discovery process. Rule 26(f) authorizes the court, after a discovery conference, to enter an order "setting limitations on discovery" and "determining other such matters . . . as are necessary for the proper management of discovery." Such a conference may be called by the court itself or upon a motion by one of the parties. The Advisory Committee Notes point out that Subdivision (f) was added to Rule 26 in 1980 because the Committee believed that discovery "abuse can best be prevented by intervention by the court as soon as abuse is threatened."

Rule 30 governs oral depositions. Rule 30(c) states: "[e]xamination and cross-examination of witnesses may proceed as permitted at the trial." Rule 30(d) gives the court the power to terminate or limit the scope of a deposition "on motion of a party" if the court finds that the deposition is being conducted in "bad faith or in such manner as unreasonably to annoy, embarrass, or oppress the deponent or party." All phases of the examination are subject to the control of the court, which has discretion to make any orders necessary to prevent the abuse of the discovery and deposition process. See, 8 Charles A. Wright & Arthur R. Miller, Federal Practice and Procedure ss 2113, 2116 (1971).

Rules 37(a)(2) and 37(a)(3) permit a party to seek, and the court to grant, an order which compels a deponent to respond to a question or to give a less evasive or more complete response.

Taken together, Rules 26(f), 30, and 37(a), along with Rule 16, which gives the court control over pre-trial case management, vest the court with broad authority and discretion to control discovery, including the conduct of depositions[1]. It is pursuant to that authority and discretion that I enter this Opinion and Order.

Plaintiff's counsel has submitted no citation, no caselaw, in support of his argument that an attorney and client may confer at their pleasure during the client's deposition. On the other hand, defendant has submitted orders from numerous courts holding that such conversations are not allowed.[2] Those courts have held that private conferences between deponents and their attorneys during the taking of a deposition are improper unless the conferences are for the purpose of determining whether a privilege should be asserted.

The United States District Court for the Eastern District of New York has adopted a similar view in a standing order: "[a]n attorney for a deponent shall not initiate a private conference with the deponent during the actual taking of a deposition, except for the purpose of determining whether a privilege should be asserted." Standing Orders of the Court on Effective Discovery in Civil Cases, 102 F.R.D. 339, 351, no. 13 (E.D.N.Y.1984). In combination with another standing order which prohibits "[o]bjections in the presence of the witness which are used to suggest an answer to the witness," id. at 351, no. 12, the judges of that district have attempted to insure that the testimony taken during a deposition is completely that of the deponent, rather than a version of that testimony which has been edited or glossed by the deponent's lawyer.

The Eastern District of New York's standing order is silent on the question of a client-deponent's initiating a private conference with his or her attorney. However, the orders in Braniff, RTC, Domestic Air, and San Juan prohibit all conferences except those discussing a privilege, regardless of who initiates them. The Rhode Island and Asbestos courts prohibited all conferences, regardless of their subject or initiator.

One of the purposes of the discovery rules in general, and the deposition rules in particular, is to elicit the facts of a case before trial. Another purpose is to even the playing field somewhat by allowing all parties access to the same information, thereby tending to prevent trial by surprise. Depositions serve another purpose as well: the memorialization, the freezing, of a witness's testimony at an early stage of the proceedings, before that witness's recollection of the

---

[1] Plaintiff's counsel argues that since the Rule 30(d) says "on motion of a party," the court is powerless to act absent such a motion. This argument is specious; the Federal Rules of Civil Procedure, and their overseers, the judiciary, are not so passively impotent.

[2] See, e.g., In re Braniff, Inc., Nos. 89-03325-BKC-6C1, 92-911, 1992 WL 261641 (Bankr.M.D.Fla. Oct. 2, 1992); RTC v. KPMG Peat Marwick, Civ.A. No. 92-1373 (E.D.Pa. Sept. 19, 1992); In re Domestic Air Transp. Antitrust Litig., 1992-1 Trade Cases P 69,731, 1990 WL 358009 (N.D.Ga. Dec. 21, 1990); In re San Juan DuPont Plaza Hotel Fire Litig., No. MDL 721, 1989 WL 168401 (D.P.R. Dec. 2, 1989); In re Rhode Island Asbestos Cases; R.I.M.L. No. 1 (D.R.I. March 15, 1982); In re Asbestos-Related Litig., No. CP-81-1 (E.D.N.C. Sept. 15, 1981).

events at issue either has faded or has been altered by intervening events, other discovery, or the helpful suggestions of lawyers.

The underlying purpose of a deposition is to find out what a witness saw, heard, or did—what the witness thinks. A deposition is meant to be a question-and-answer conversation between the deposing lawyer and the witness. There is no proper need for the witness's own lawyer to act as an intermediary, interpreting questions, deciding which questions the witness should answer,[3] and helping the witness to formulate answers. The witness comes to the deposition to testify, not to indulge in a parody of Charlie McCarthy, with lawyers coaching or bending the witness's words to mold a legally convenient record. It is the witness—not the lawyer—who is the witness. As an advocate, the lawyer is free to frame those facts in a manner favorable to the client, and also to make favorable and creative arguments of law. But the lawyer is not entitled to be creative with the facts. Rather, a lawyer must accept the facts as they develop. Therefore, I hold that a lawyer and client do not have an absolute right to confer during the course of the client's deposition.

Concern has been expressed as to the client's right to counsel and to due process. A lawyer, of course, has the right, if not the duty,[4] to prepare a client for a deposition. But once a deposition begins, the right to counsel is somewhat tempered by the underlying goal of our discovery rules: getting to the truth. Under Rule 30(c), depositions generally are to be conducted under the same testimonial rules as are trials. During a civil trial, a witness and his or her lawyer are not permitted to confer at their pleasure during the witness's testimony[5]. Once a witness has been prepared and has taken the stand, that witness is on his or her own.

The same is true at a deposition. The fact that there is no judge in the room to prevent private conferences does not mean that such conferences should or may occur. The underlying

---

[3] I note that under Rule 32(d)(3)(A), objections to the competency, relevancy, or materiality of deposition testimony generally are preserved for trial. Therefore, counsel should not repeatedly interrupt the deposition to make these objections. Of course, the witness's counsel is free to object on the ground that a question asks for an answer which is protected by a privilege, and to make objections which would be waived if not raised immediately. See, Fed.R.Civ.P. 32(d)(3)(B).

[4] "A lawyer shall provide competent representation to a client. Competent representation requires the legal knowledge, skill, thoroughness and preparation necessary for the representation." Pennsylvania Rule of Professional Conduct 1.1.

[5] Lawyers, of course, do not often attempt to interrupt the questioning of their clients at trial to have private conferences, probably because they think that doing so would tend to diminish the witness-client's credibility. Some district courts have ordered lawyers and witness-clients not to confer even during lunch and overnight breaks in the witness-client's testimony. In Aiello v. City of Wilmington, 623 F.2d 845, 858- 59 (3d Cir.1980), the district court, because of its concern over "witness coaching," ordered the plaintiff and his counsel not to communicate during breaks in the plaintiff's cross-examination. The Third Circuit did not decide, and to this court's knowledge still has not decided, whether such an order might violate the right to counsel.

reason for preventing private conferences is still present: they tend, at the very least, to give the appearance of obstructing the truth.

[3] These considerations apply also to conferences initiated by the witness, as opposed to the witness's lawyer. To allow private conferences initiated by the witness would be to allow the witness to listen to the question, ask his or her lawyer for the answer, and then parrot the lawyer's response. Again, this is not what depositions are all about—or, at least, it is not what they are supposed to be all about. If the witness does not understand the question, or needs some language further defined or some documents further explained, the witness can ask the deposing lawyer to clarify or further explain the question[6]. After all, the lawyer who asked the question is in a better position to explain the question than is the witness's own lawyer. There is simply no qualitative distinction between private conferences initiated by a lawyer and those initiated by a witness. Neither should occur.

These rules also apply during recesses. Once the deposition has begun, the preparation period is over and the deposing lawyer is entitled to pursue the chosen line of inquiry without interjection by the witness's counsel. Private conferences are barred during the deposition, and the fortuitous occurrence of a coffee break, lunch break, or evening recess is no reason to change the rules. Otherwise, the same problems would persist. A clever lawyer or witness who finds that a deposition is going in an undesired or unanticipated direction could simply insist on a short recess to discuss the unanticipated yet desired answers, thereby circumventing the prohibition on private conferences. Therefore, I hold that conferences between witness and lawyer are prohibited both during the deposition and during recesses.[7]

The same reasoning applies to conferences about documents shown to the witness during the deposition. When the deposing attorney presents a document to a witness at a deposition, that attorney is entitled to have the witness, and the witness alone, answer questions about the document. The witness's lawyer should be given a copy of the document for his or her own inspection, but there is no valid reason why the lawyer and the witness should have to confer about the document before the witness answers questions about it[8]. If the witness does not recall

---

[6]At the beginning of the deposition, the deposing lawyer should explain to the witness, as did Mr. Stewart here, that the witness should feel free to ask for clarification at any time during the deposition.

[7]To the extent that such conferences do occur, in violation of this Opinion and Order, I am of the view that these conferences are not covered by the attorney-client privilege, at least as to what is said by the lawyer to the witness. Therefore, any such conferences are fair game for inquiry by the deposing attorney to ascertain whether there has been any coaching and, if so, what.

[8]This approach is consistent with Federal Rule of Evidence 613(a), which provides: "[i]n examining a witness concerning a prior statement made by the witness, whether written or not, the statement need not be shown nor its contents disclosed to the witness at that time, but on request the same shall be shown or disclosed to opposing counsel." The Advisory Committee Notes observe that "[t]he provision for disclosure to counsel is designed to protect against unwarranted insinuations that a statement has been made when the fact is to the

having seen the document before or does not understand the document, the witness may ask the deposing lawyer for some additional information, or the witness may simply testify to the lack of knowledge or understanding. But there need not be an off-the-record conference between witness and lawyer in order to ascertain whether the witness understands the document or a pending question about the document.

As mentioned above, the majority of federal courts which have issued deposition guidelines have held that a private conference between witness and attorney is permissible if the purpose of the conference is to decide whether to assert a privilege. With this exception I agree. Since the assertion of a privilege is a proper, and very important, objection during a deposition, it makes sense to allow the witness the opportunity to consult with counsel about whether to assert a privilege. Further, privileges are violated not only by the admission of privileged evidence at trial, but by the very disclosures themselves. Thus, it is important that the witness be fully informed of his or her rights before making a statement which might reveal privileged information. However, when such a conference occurs, the conferring attorney should place on the record the fact that the conference occurred, the subject of the conference, and the decision reached as to whether to assert a privilege.

Having discussed off-the-record witness-coaching, I now turn to a related concern: on-the-record witness-coaching through suggestive objections. Without guidelines on suggestive objections, the spirit of the prohibition against private conferences could be flouted by a lawyer's making of lengthy objections which contain information suggestive of an answer to a pending question. The Supreme Court has recently addressed the issue of suggestive objections in the Proposed Amendments to the Federal Rules of Civil Procedure and Forms, H.R.Doc. No. 74, 103rd Cong., 1st Sess., at 50–52 (Apr. 22, 1993). Proposed Amended Rule 30(d) reads: (1) Any objection to evidence during a deposition shall be stated concisely and in a non-argumentative and non-suggestive manner. A party may instruct a deponent not to answer only when necessary to preserve a privilege, to enforce a limitation on evidence directed by the court, or to present a motion pursuant to paragraph (3).[9]

(2) By order or local rule, the court may limit the time permitted for the conduct of a deposition, but shall allow additional time consistent with Rule 26(b)(2) if needed for a fair

---

contrary." Thus, the requirement that counsel be shown the document exists only to assure counsel that the document actually exists, not to allow counsel to prepare the witness to testify about it. Rule 613(a) is contrary to the rule in Queen Caroline's Case, 129 Eng.Rep. 976 (1820). In that case, English judges advised that, before being cross-examined about a document, a witness must be shown the document and given the opportunity to read the relevant portion. The rule proved so obstructive that it was abolished by Parliament in 1854. 17 & 18 Vict., ch. 125, s 24 (1854) (Eng.). See, John W. Strong et al., 1 McCormick on Evidence s 28 (4th ed. 1992).

[9]Paragraph (3) is substantially similar to the current Rule 30(d), which governs motions to terminate or limit examination because of bad faith, unreasonableness, annoyance, embarrassment, or oppression.

examination of the deponent or if the deponent or another party impedes or delays the examination. If the court finds such an impediment, delay, or other conduct that has frustrated the fair examination of the deponent, it may impose upon the persons responsible an appropriate sanction, including the reasonable costs and attorney's fees incurred by any parties as a result thereof. The Committee Notes following the proposed amended rule contain the following observations: Depositions frequently have been unduly prolonged, if not unfairly frustrated, by lengthy objections and colloquy, often suggesting how the deponent should respond. . . . [O]bjections . . . should be limited to those that under Rule 32(d)(3) might be waived if not made at that time. . . . [O]ther objections can . . . be raised for the first time at trial and therefore should be kept at a minimum during a deposition. Directions to a deponent not to answer a question can be even more disruptive than objections. . . . In general, counsel should not engage in any conduct during a deposition that would not be allowed in the presence of a judicial officer. The making of an excessive number of objections may itself constitute sanctionable conduct. Proposed Amendments, H.R.Doc. No. 74, at 261-63.

The proposed amendments and committee notes aptly observe that objections and colloquy by lawyers tend to disrupt the question-and-answer rhythm of a deposition and obstruct the witness's testimony. Since most objections, such as those grounded on relevance or materiality, are preserved for trial, they need not be made.[10] [FN10] As for those few objections which would be waived if not made immediately, they should be stated pithily. See, Fed.R.Civ.P. 32(d)(3).

The Federal Rules of Evidence contain no provision allowing lawyers to interrupt the trial testimony of a witness to make a statement. Such behavior should likewise be prohibited at depositions, since it tends to obstruct the taking of the witness's testimony. It should go without saying that lawyers are strictly prohibited from making any comments, either on or off the record, which might suggest or limit a witness's answer to an unobjectionable question.

In short, depositions are to be limited to what they were and are intended to be: question-and-answer sessions between a lawyer and a witness aimed at uncovering the facts in a lawsuit. When a deposition becomes something other than that because of the strategic interruptions, suggestions, statements, and arguments of counsel, it not only becomes

---

[10]I also note that a favorite objection or interjection of lawyers is, "I don't understand the question; therefore the witness doesn't understand the question." This is not a proper objection. If the witness needs clarification, the witness may ask the deposing lawyer for clarification. A lawyer's purported lack of understanding is not a proper reason to interrupt a deposition. In addition, counsel are not permitted to state on the record their interpretations of questions, since those interpretations are irrelevant and often suggestive of a particularly desired answer.

unnecessarily long, but it ceases to serve the purpose of the Federal Rules of Civil Procedure: to find and fix[11] the truth.

Depositions are the factual battleground where the vast majority of litigation actually takes place. It may safely be said that Rule 30 has spawned a veritable cottage industry. The significance of depositions has grown geometrically over the years to the point where their pervasiveness now dwarfs both the time spent and the facts learned at the actual trial—assuming there is a trial, which there usually is not[12]. The pretrial tail now wags the trial dog. Thus, it is particularly important that this discovery device not be abused. Counsel should never forget that even though the deposition may be taking place far from a real courtroom, with no black-robed overseer peering down upon them, as long as the deposition is conducted under the caption of this court and proceeding under the authority of the rules of this court, counsel are operating as officers of this court. They should comport themselves accordingly; should they be tempted to stray, they should remember that this judge is but a phone call away.

An Order containing guidelines for the conduct of the depositions of parties and other witnesses represented by counsel in this case follows.

ORDER

AND NOW, this 29th day of July, 1993, upon consideration of the oral arguments and letter briefs of the parties regarding the dispute over the conduct of counsel at depositions, it is ORDERED that the following guidelines for discovery depositions are hereby imposed:

1. At the beginning of the deposition, deposing counsel shall instruct the witness to ask deposing counsel, rather than the witness's own counsel, for clarifications, definitions, or explanations of any words, questions, or documents presented during the course of the deposition. The witness shall abide by these instructions.

2. All objections, except those which would be waived if not made at the deposition under Federal Rules of Civil Procedure 32(d)(3)(B), and those necessary to assert a privilege, to enforce a limitation on evidence directed by the court, or to present a motion pursuant to Federal Rules of Civil Procedure 30(d), shall be preserved. Therefore, those objections need not and shall not be made during the course of depositions.

---

[11]"Fix" in the sense of firmly stabilizing (such as a photographic image), rather than bending or muting the record to make it more factually comfy—as in to "fix" a prize fight, or a jury.

[12]From October 1, 1991, to September 30, 1992, 8,771 civil cases terminated in this judicial district. Of those, only 337, or 3.8 percent, actually went to trial. Annual Report of the Director of the Administrative Office of the United States Courts—1992, at Table C 4A. The reality is that what is learned at depositions becomes the factual basis upon which most cases are disposed of not by trial, but by settlement. Thus, if those "facts" get skewed, the risk is grave that so also will the quality of justice.

3. Counsel shall not direct or request that a witness not answer a question, unless that counsel has objected to the question on the ground that the answer is protected by a privilege or a limitation on evidence directed by the court.

4. Counsel shall not make objections or statements which might suggest an answer to a witness. Counsels' statements when making objections should be succinct and verbally economical, stating the basis of the objection and nothing more.

5. Counsel and their witness-clients shall not engage in private, off-the-record conferences during depositions or during breaks or recesses, except for the purpose of deciding whether to assert a privilege.

6. Any conferences which occur pursuant to, or in violation of, guideline (5) are a proper subject for inquiry by deposing counsel to ascertain whether there has been any witness-coaching and, if so, what.

7. Any conferences which occur pursuant to, or in violation of, guideline (5) shall be noted on the record by the counsel who participated in the conference. The purpose and outcome of the conference shall also be noted on the record.

8. Deposing counsel shall provide to the witness's counsel a copy of all documents shown to the witness during the deposition. The copies shall be provided either before the deposition begins or contemporaneously with the showing of each document to the witness. The witness and the witness's counsel do not have the right to discuss documents privately before the witness answers questions about them.

9. Depositions shall otherwise be conducted in compliance with the Opinion which accompanies this Order.